Clear and Present Dangers:
The U.S. Military and the War on Drugs in the Andes

October 1991

Washington Office on Latin America

110 Maryland Avenue, NE
Washington, DC   20002-5696 • U.S.A.
tel 202-544-8045 • fax 202-546-5288

ISBN 0-929513-20-7

The Washington Office on Latin America (WOLA) is a non-governmental organization supported by private foundations, religious organizations and individual donors. Contributions are tax-deductible.

Copies of this report may be obtained for $12.00 each. Please include $1.75 postage/handling for first copy, $0.75 for each additional. Submit book orders to:

Washington Office on Latin America
110 Maryland Avenue, NE
Washington, DC 20002-5696 • U.S.A.
tel 202-544-8045
fax 202-546-5288
email (PeaceNet): "wola"

Cover photo: Colombian National Police on anti-narcotics raid in Huila mountains. Photo by Timothy Ross Picture Group.

TABLE OF CONTENTS

PREFACE

Since its creation in 1974, the Washington Office on Latin America (WOLA) has been concerned about militarism in this hemisphere. Beginning in 1940s and 1950s, strong military-to-military relationships were developed between the U.S. Southern Command (SouthCom) in Panama and the national security forces in the region. These forces, including the police, were "modernized" under U.S. tutelage in many countries. During the period of the Alliance for Progress, announced in 1961, U.S. aid and training particularly emphasized counter-insurgency operations.

During the 1970s WOLA joined others in supporting congressionally-mandated human rights conditions on U.S. foreign assistance, including military aid. This legislation had the effect during the Carter administration of cutting such U.S. aid to the military dictatorships that then predominated in Latin America. When elected civilian governments replaced these dictatorships throughout the region during the 1980s, U.S. military aid, and military-to-military relationships, again increased -- first to Central America and then, at the end of the decade, to the Andean countries. The impact of LIC doctrine in Central America (including aid to the Nicaraguan "contras") is well known. The application of that doctrine to the Andes in the "war on drugs" is now underway -- in a multifaceted five-year $2.2 billion program -- and that is the subject of this report.

The Andean Strategy encompasses a range of specific initiatives, including economic assistance, but its military component is crucial and central. WOLA has for several years analyzed different aspects of the "war on drugs," particularly its potential effects on human rights and political violence in the Andean region. This report presents some of that broader analysis in synthesis but focuses primarily on the unfolding military component, both on U.S. activities and on the incipient response from the national security forces of the Andean countries themselves. It does not attempt to provide a comprehensive examination of U.S. drug policy or of other efforts -- through the Organization of American States and the United Nations, for example -- to address the problems of international drug trafficking in the hemisphere. Rather, it aims to contribute to a vitally-needed public debate, in the Andes as well as in the United States, of the character and potential consequences of the militarized drug war.

The research and writing of this report was primarily carried out by Charles Call, a WOLA Associate. WOLA Senior Associate Coletta Youngers contributed to the research and the writing. Alex Wilde, Executive Director of WOLA, edited the report. Other WOLA staff provided much helpful assistance in its preparation, particularly South American Team Assistant Susana Cárdenas.

This report would not have been possible without the help and cooperation of many other individuals and organizations. WOLA is grateful to the National Security Archive, and especially to analyst Kate Doyle, for use of the Archive's extensive materials. We want to express our particular gratitude to the human rights organizations of Colombia, Peru, and Bolivia for their invaluable and courageous assistance in providing information which in some cases has placed them -- and continues to place them -- in danger.

The research for this report draws on interviews with numerous government officials in Washington, D.C., at U.S. Embassies in Peru, Bolivia, and Colombia, at the U.S. Southern Command in Panama, and at the Center for Low Intensity Conflict at Langley Air Force Base in Virginia. Where possible, government officials and others have been identified by name and office. Where sources are not identified, it is always because such sources spoke on "background," i.e., on the condition that they not be identified by name or office.

WOLA wishes to thank all of the U.S. government officials who agreed to be interviewed (in some cases, several times) for this report: administration officials of the Department of Defense, the Department of State, and the U.S. Drug Enforcement Administration; and staff members of the U.S. Congress.

Several people provided comments on initial drafts of this study: Peter Andreas, J. Samuel Fitch, Peter Hakim, Jo Ann Kawell, Rachel Neild, Tina Rosenberg, Peter Sollis, Senate staff member Hal Lippman, and a senior congressional staff member who has chosen to remain anonymous. The report is better for their timely and thoughtful criticisms, but none of them bears any responsibility for its final form or conclusions.

Finally, WOLA is grateful to the J. Roderick MacArthur Foundation and the Ruth Mott Fund for specific support for research and publication of this report, as well as to the C.S. Fund, Ford Foundation, and the General Service Foundation for general support for WOLA's work on human rights in the Andes.

ACRONYMS AND ABBREVIATIONS

CBRN	Caribbean Basin Radar Network
CIA	U.S. Central Intelligence Agency
CINCSO	Commander-in-Chief Southern Command
CLIC	Center for Low Intensity Conflict, U.S. Army-Air Force
CNP	Colombia National Police
DAN	Anti-narcotics Directorate, Colombia National Police
DEA	U.S. Drug Enforcement Administration
DOD	U.S. Department of Defense
DOS	U.S. Department of State
DSAA	U.S. Defense Security Assistance Agency
ELN	National Liberation Army
ESF	Economic Support Funds
FARC	Revolutionary Armed Forces of Colombia
FBI	U.S. Federal Bureau of Investigations
FMF	Foreign Military Financing
IMET	International Military Education and Training
INCSR	International Narcotics Control Strategy Report
INM	Bureau of International Narcotics Matters, U.S. State Department
LIC	Low Intensity Conflict
MTT	Mobile Training Team
ONDCP	Office of National Drug Control Policy
SouthCom	U.S. Southern Command
TAT	Tactical Analysis Team
UHV	Upper Huallaga Valley (Peru)
UMOPAR	Bolivian Rural Mobile Patrol Unit (Police)
U.S. AID	U.S. Agency for International Development
USSOCOM	U.S. Special Operations Command

Tables and Diagrams

EXECUTIVE SUMMARY

The drug war has replaced the Cold War as the central U.S. military mission in the hemisphere. As part of President Bush's "Andean strategy" --a multi-faceted effort to reduce the flow of cocaine into the United States -- the Pentagon has launched a massive anti-narcotics program which begins in the Andes and then moves to Central America and the rest of South America. In 1990, the Panama-based U.S. Southern Command (SouthCom) declared drugs its "number one priority," and its budget for anti-drug activities in Latin America had risen to $100 million by FY 1991. The Pentagon is installing a sophisticated regional intelligence network which draws on satellites, air reconnaissance flights, and radar based in 18 countries.

Rather than using U.S. troops directly in operations, the Andean strategy depends on getting Latin American military and police forces more involved in the drug war and increasing their capabilities. In Colombia, Peru, and Bolivia, all three services -- Army, Navy, and Air Force -- have now signed on to the drug war. Drug-related training of police forces is ongoing in all three countries, while training of army personnel is underway in Bolivia and Colombia and about to begin in Peru. U.S. plans include improving the intelligence-gathering capabilities of Andean militaries and police, providing them with millions of dollars of equipment, and giving them advice in planning and carrying out operations. Small teams of U.S. military specialists already select targets, plan raids, and coordinate operations carried out by U.S. DEA and Andean police and military forces. In addition, the Central Intelligence Agency acknowledges having shifted its priorities to become more heavily involved in the drug war in Latin America.

Reflecting post-Cold War realities, the Andean region has supplanted Central America as the main locus of U.S. military activity in the hemisphere. Colombia, Bolivia and Peru are slated to receive more U.S. military assistance over the three-year period between FY 1990 and FY 1992 than all of Central America. Although little U.S. equipment has yet arrived, U.S. drug-related military assistance allocated to Colombia, Bolivia, and Peru increased from less than $5 million in FY 1988 to over $140 million in FY 1990 -- a level which is likely to persist through 1992. In FY 1990, Colombia surpassed El Salvador as the hemisphere's top recipient of military aid including "drawdown" equipment. U.S. military assistance to Bolivia in FY 1990 represented a 41% increase in the Defense Ministry's budget.

U.S. military officials acknowledge that the counter-narcotics mission serves important interests of the U.S. military in Latin America at a critical

1

historical juncture. It gives the military a new mission in the hemisphere just as the Cold War has changed the nature of U.S. military strategy worldwide. It also converges with new post-Cold War opportunities to strengthen bilateral relations with the armed forces of Latin America. And, unlike new anti-drug roles on the domestic side such as logistical support for law enforcement agencies and border interdiction (which the military has resisted as detracting from its central mission), it converges with previous low-intensity conflict roles in Latin America. These institutional developments indicate that the military component of the drug war is not likely to be a quick, surgical operation, but rather a long-term, comprehensive effort. SouthCom is already seeking to expand the drug war throughout the hemisphere.

The military thrust of the U.S. strategy has been resisted by the Andean governments themselves. Although all three governments have now accepted military aid in exchange for U.S. economic assistance, they continue to assign quite different priority to the drug war than the United States. In Peru and Bolivia, armed forces personnel have fired on local police and DEA agents. Colombia strongly opposes a high-profile role for U.S. personnel, and Bolivian and Peruvian governments consistently claim that offering rural coca growers positive incentives of viable alternative crops will be more effective than militarized interdiction and eradication.

The "Drug War" as Low-Intensity Conflict

U.S. military documents, presented in Chapter 3, illustrate that the Pentagon views the counter-drug mission as the latest form of low-intensity conflict, one which consciously draws on the strategy and tactics of counter-insurgency. While the targets of the Andean programs include "new" enemies -- cocaine producers and traffickers -- the "old" enemies of Marxist insurgents are explicitly part of anti-narcotics programs in Peru and Colombia. Under what many call the "narco-guerrilla theory," administration officials insist that anti-narcotics monies be used to fight insurgents who are alleged to have "inextricable links" with drug traffickers.

Although administration officials assure Congress that anti-drug funds will only be used against insurgent activities which are tied to drug trafficking, realities in the region indicate otherwise. Top Peruvian and Colombian armed forces commanders have stated that they plan to utilize anti-narcotics monies for their top priority -- counter-insurgency -- and Congressional studies have found that effective mechanisms are lacking to monitor how U.S. military assistance is actually used.

2

The "narco-guerrilla" theory has been questioned by experts in the Andean countries and in the United States. The theory fits poorly in Colombia, where drug mafias have been more closely associated with right-wing paramilitary death squads than leftist insurgents, and where Colombian officials acknowledge that the military is marginal to anti-drug operations. Even in Peru, where Sendero Luminoso guerrillas have a powerful presence in the coca-producing Upper Huallaga Valley, Peruvian military leaders themselves have warned that it is impossible to fight guerrillas and traffickers at the same time. Peruvian analysts claim that, as peasants seek protection from coca repression programs, support for the Shining Path guerrillas has increased. According to Hernando de Soto, a key adviser to the Fujimori government, "our military tells us that militarizing the drug war will give Sendero an army of 250,000 [coca-growing] farmers."

Why the Strategy Cannot Work

There is widespread agreement that the Andean strategy has not met its objectives to date. Administration officials claim that progress is being made in cowing cartel leaders into surrender, in strengthening governmental law enforcement efforts, and in curbing coca cultivation. However, they also acknowledge that in the Andean region the United States has failed to achieve its chief two-year goal of reducing cocaine supply to the United States by 15%. In fact, U.S. Drug Enforcement Administration agents report that production in South America increased in 1990 by 28%. And DEA agents estimate that coca production will increase in 1991 by another 10%, reaching record levels. Despite the fact that the Medellín cartel's violence against the state has been dramatically reduced, drug trafficking continues. The Cali cartel has become the largest in the world, and Colombian officials report that the Medellín cartels' top leaders continue to direct trafficking operations from their cells. Furthermore, Interpol and DEA officials say that cocaine processing and trafficking centers have expanded in Bolivia, Venezuela, Brazil, Peru, and Ecuador.

In the face of these results, the administration is extending its drug war to other countries in the hemisphere and dedicating more resources to international anti-narcotics activities. U.S. military officials are pressing governments throughout Latin America to get their armed forces involved in anti-narcotics activities, and the United States has begun providing drug-related support to police and/or military forces in Guatemala, Honduras, Costa Rica, Ecuador, Argentina, Brazil, Paraguay, and Venezuela. Yet there is overwhelming evidence that the strategy will not alleviate drug abuse and drug-related violence in U.S. cities. Because the source-country portion of the cocaine industry contributes less than 15% to the final street price, experts say that a reduction of even 50% of cocaine shipments to the U.S. would raise the street price by only 3%. In addition, DEA officials acknowledge that successful repression efforts are likely to spread cocaine production to other countries, thus guaranteeing a steady supply of the drug to the U.S. market.

The Negative Consequences

Not only is the military component of the Andean strategy unlikely to work, but it may well have many of the same negative consequences of U.S.-sponsored counter-insurgency in countries such as El Salvador. In the Andes, the U.S. has allied itself with regimes whose armed forces and police engage in widespread and egregious human rights violations. In Colombia and Peru, these forces are involved routinely in extrajudicial executions, disappearances, torture, massacres, and other abuses. Despite the Bush administration's increased attention to human rights in U.S. military training programs, security assistance is going directly to counter-insurgency campaigns in advance of any meaningful reforms.

In addition, U.S. anti-narcotics policy could well weaken civilian leaders by increasing the resources and profile of armed forces in the region. In Bolivia and Peru, where militaries turned over power only a decade ago, academics and politicians alike fear that widening the internal security role of the armed forces may endanger civilian rule and increase the impunity with which they commit human rights abuse. Thirty years ago the United States pressed Latin American militaries to take on internal insurgencies as a national security mission. Now, as then, the U.S. may be playing a decisive role in legitimating a new military mission that will have destructive political and social ramifications in the region.

The extraordinary enhancement of intelligence-gathering could have particularly harmful consequences. During Latin America's military dictatorships of the 1960s and '70s, intelligence units were the source of the worst manifestations of state terror. The character of intelligence and the uses to which it is put depend on whether those in command answer to democratic civilian authority. Andean security forces are unaccountable to such authority -- and endemically unwilling to distinguish between armed rebellion and legal political opposition.

Finally, in Bolivia and Peru, where the bulk of coca leaf is produced, the Andean strategy may well fuel political violence by closing off economic alternatives to farmers who face a desperate situation. In Bolivia, sectors across the political spectrum, including all opposition parties and the Catholic church, have opposed the "militarization" of the

4

drug war. Some coca-growers federations have called for self-defense groups, and violent confrontations between anti-narcotics forces and local populations have already occurred in both Peru and Bolivia.

The clear and present dangers of the militarized Andean strategy have not yet been faced in a public debate that is now imperative, both in the United States and in the Andes. Nor has the U.S. Congress squarely faced the issue of military aid for Andean counter-insurgencies. Such aid must be debated in its own terms, not disguised as part of a different war, the war on drugs.

The choice is not between the current strategy and "doing nothing," but there are real limits to what the U.S. can -- and should -- do in the supplier countries. For the serious problems that Andean governments face from drug trafficking, the United States can offer assistance if it confronts those problems on their own terms. Such assistance, however, will only be useful to the degree that it reinforces the efforts Andean governments themselves make -- to address the deep inequities in their economies and achieve more stable and productive development, and to remedy the fundamental weaknesses of their justice systems in confronting widespread violence and impunity. Ultimately, however, U.S. drug-related problems are rooted in domestic conditions and will not be solved by strengthening Andean military or even police forces. Instead, as numerous experts and Pentagon officials have suggested, the United States should channel increasing resources to the demand side here at home.

CHAPTER 1

THE BUSH ADMINISTRATION'S "WAR ON DRUGS"

Chapter Summary

The Bush administration's "war on drugs" is not the first drug war in U.S. history. In 1968, President Nixon declared a "war on drugs," establishing a series of offices for anti-narcotics coordination and enforcement, including what in 1973 became known as the Drug Enforcement Administration (DEA). In the 1980s, the Reagan administration also waged a war on drugs, declaring drug trafficking a threat to national security. These recent policies have historical precedents in lower profile anti-narcotics efforts, such as anti-cocaine and anti-opium policies of the early twentieth century and anti-cocaine policies toward Peru during the 1940s and 50s.[1]

The Bush administration's drug war, however, differs from previous efforts in important ways. The current version is the highest profile, most expensive anti-narcotics program in U.S. history. Spending on all federal anti-drug programs has increased from $6.4 billion in 1988 to over $11 billion in Fiscal Year (FY) 1992. The Bush administration has taken far more initiative than did the Reagan administration in drug control efforts and has staked more political capital on the issue. And while events in the Persian Gulf and the Soviet Union have eclipsed the drug war in the media, drugs remain a major issue of domestic policy.

In addition, Bush's drug war now tops the U.S. national security agenda in Latin America. With the end of the Cold War, the spread of civilian rule in Latin America, and the progress of peace processes in Central America, economic issues have taken top priority both in Latin America and in the new administration's policy toward the region.[2] However, U.S. security policy continues to have a significant impact on the hemisphere, and the administration has shifted its security concerns from Central American wars of national liberation to the Andean region and the dangers of drug trafficking. The United States justified its 1989 invasion of Panama partly in the name of the drug war, and U.S. military documents now speak of measuring security threats in "kilos" rather than in "megatons."[3]

---

[1] See William O. Walker III, "The Bush Administration's Andean Strategy in Historical Perspective," paper presented at a conference on "U.S.-Latin American Relations in the 1990s," in Miami, Florida, 13-15 June 1991.

[2] The administration's Enterprise for the Americas Initiative and its strong advocacy of a Free Trade Agreement with Mexico are emblematic of its concern with economic issues.

[3] U.S. Southern Command, Southern Theater Strategy, February 1991.

Most significantly, the Bush drug war has given more weight to attacking the cocaine industry at its "source" and has sharply escalated the reliance on U.S. and foreign armed forces to fight the drug war. A number of factors lie behind this new emphasis. As domestic pressure for action against drug abuse rose throughout the 1980s, Congress and the administration expressed frustration at the failure of federal anti-narcotics measures. Members of Congress from both parties called for the increased use of the military. And within "source countries," U.S. officials encountered a host of obstacles, including fears that paramilitary police efforts were inadequate in the face of well-armed cartels, especially in situations where civil conflicts complicated the scenario. All of these factors help explain the turn to the military under the Bush administration.

I. THE ANDEAN STRATEGY

U.S. anti-narcotics policy in the Andes is part of an increased anti-drug effort on several fronts. The federal narcotics control strategy includes both supply-side measures such as domestic law enforcement activities, border interdiction, and all international programs, as well as expanded demand-side programs in treatment, education and prevention. The program is coordinated by the "Drug Czar" (now former Florida governor Robert Martinez), who heads the Office of National Drug Control Policy (ONDCP).

Since before 1988, one of the most controversial features of the federal National Drug Control Strategy has been its emphasis on supply-side measures, rather than demand-side programs. The supply/demand breakdown has remained at roughly 70/30 from 1988 through 1992 (See Table 1.A). Congressional bodies define "supply-side" measures as not simply efforts in foreign countries and border interdiction activities, but also domestic law enforcement efforts.[4] "Demand-side programs" includes treatment, education, and prevention programs.

Anti-narcotics programs in Latin America comprise a small percentage of the growing federal anti-drug budget. The overall federal anti-narcotics budget has increased by 82% under the Bush administration (from $6.4 billion in FY 1988 to a requested $11.7 billion in FY 1992). In FY 1991, "international initiatives" (including anti-narcotics programs in Latin America) comprised only 6% of total federal anti-narcotics spending.[5] Yet international

---

[4] See House Committee on Government Operations, "U.S. Anti-Narcotics Activities in the Andean Region," Thirty-Eighth Report, November 1990, p. 6. Based on ONDCP figures, January 1990, p. 100.

[5] Ibid.

Table 1.A
SUPPLY/DEMAND RATIO:
TOTAL U.S. FEDERAL DRUG CONTROL BUDGET
FY 1988 - FY 1992

	1988	1989	1990	1991	1992
Supply*	70.3%	71.2%	69.9%	67.9%	68.6%
Demand	25.9	25.2	26.6	28.0	27.2
Research (both)	3.8	3.6	3.5	4.1	4.2
Total	100.0%	100.0%	100.0%	100.0%	100.0%

* Supply figures include both domestic and international supply-reduction efforts.

SOURCE: ONDCP. Calculated from "National Drug Control Budget By Function," Budget Authority figures (FY 1988-FY 1990 actual; FY 1991 estimated; FY 1992 requested), *National Drug Control Strategy -- Budget Summary*, White House, February 1991, pp. 216-219.

spending has increased dramatically, from $250 million in FY 1989 to $779 million in FY 1992.[6] Between FY 1990 and FY 1991, the budget for international initiatives grew more rapidly than the rest of the anti-drug budget.[7]

In September 1989, President Bush announced the "Andean strategy," the administration's blueprint for attacking cocaine supply where it is produced.[8] Despite its small size in the anti-drug budget, the Andean strategy is considered a key component of overall federal anti-narcotics programs and the centerpiece of U.S. international drug control efforts. The inter-agency program targets the countries which account for almost 100% of the cocaine supply to the United States: Colombia, Peru and Bolivia.[9]

The stated long-term goal of the Andean strategy is to achieve "a major reduction in the supply of cocaine from these countries" by working "with the host governments to disrupt and destroy the growing, processing and

---

[6] "International initiatives" includes narcotics-related security and economic assistance, as well as the budgets for drug-related activities of U.S. agencies such as the Department of State, the Department of Defense and the Drug Enforcement Administration. See Appendix B, National Drug Control Strategy, November 1991 and September 1989.

[7] House Committee on Government Operations, "Thirty-Eighth Report," op cit., p. 6.

[8] President Bush referred only to the "Andean Initiative" in his September 1989 speech. Since then, however, the term "Andean strategy" has been applied by the administration to the overall Andean anti-narcotics efforts described in the speech, which encompass the Andean Initiative.

[9] Since the "Andean strategy" announcement, cocaine production has spread to neighboring countries such as Brazil and Venezuela.

transportation of coca and coca products."[10]   The strategy's quantifiable objectives are to reduce the availability of cocaine in the United States by 15% by the end of 1991 -- and 60% by 1999.[11]

The chief instrument of the Andean strategy is a five-year, $2.2 billion foreign assistance package known as the "Andean Initiative." The Andean Initiative envisions $1.11 billion in economic aid and $1.04 billion in military and law enforcement support to the governments of Colombia, Peru and Bolivia between FY 1990 and FY 1994 (see Table 1.B). The aid package is viewed as key to the Andean strategy's current four "near-term goals":

(1) "To strengthen the political commitment and institutional capability of the Governments of Colombia, Peru, and Bolivia" to disrupt, and ultimately dismantle, trafficking organizations;

(2) "To increase the effectiveness of law enforcement and security activities of the three countries against the cocaine trade. This involves providing law enforcement and military assistance to enable them to fight the traffickers in remote and inaccessible areas in which drug production activities often take place";

(3) "To inflict significant damage on the trafficking organizations that predominate within the three countries..."; and

(4) "To strengthen and diversify the legitimate economies of the Andean nations to enable them to overcome the destabilizing effects of eliminating cocaine, a major source of income."[12]

The Andean strategy marks a break with past policies by sharply expanding the role of the Department of Defense and the Central Intelligence Agency. An array of other U.S. agencies are involved. The State Department holds responsibility for overseeing narcotics control programs in foreign countries. A "Country Team" comprised of representatives from various U.S. agencies and under the Ambassador's charge coordinates all U.S. anti-narcotics activities in each country. The DEA, which maintains permanent agents in each country plus temporary agents in Peru, Bolivia and Ecuador, carries out law enforcement support activities abroad. In addition, the Border

---

[10] ONDCP, National Drug Control Strategy, January 1990, p. 49.

[11] ONCDP, National Drug Control Strategy, March 1990.

[12] ONDCP, National Drug Control Strategy, February 1991, pp. 78-79. These are the strategy's goals as of June 1991: the goals have been continually modified since the first national strategy in 1989.

Table 1.B

	FY 1989 Actual	FY 1990 Estimate 1/	FY 1991 Request	FY 1992 Plan	FY 1993 Plan	FY 1994 Plan	Total 5-Year Plan
ANDEAN STRATEGY NARCOTICS-RELATED FUNDING (in millions of dollars)							
COLOMBIA:							
Military Assistance 2	$8.6	$40.3	$60.5	$60.5	$60.5	$60 5	$282.3
Economic Assistance	$0.0	$3.6	$50.0	$50.0	$50.0	$50.0	$203.6
Law Enforcement 3/	$10.0	$20.0	$20.0	$20.0	$20.0	$20.0	$100.0
DEA Support	$4.2	$4.4	$4.4	$4.4	$4.4	$4.4	$22.0
TOTAL	$22.8	$68.3	$134.9	$134.9	$134.9	$134.9	$607.9
PERU:							
Military Assistance 2	$2.6	$36.5	$39.9	$39.9	$39.9	$39.9	$196.1
Economic Assistance	$1.3	$4.3	$63.1	$103.1	$103.1	$103.1	$376.7
Law Enforcement	$10.5	$19.0	$19.0	$19.0	$19.0	$19.0	$95.0
DEA Support	$4.3	$6.8	$6.8	$6.8	$6.8	$6.8	$34.0
TOTAL	$18.7	$66.6	$128.8	$168.8	$168.8	$168.8	$701.8
BOLIVIA:							
Military Assistance 2	$5.8	$33.7	$40.9	$40.9	$40.9	$40.9	$197.3
Economic Assistance	$4.0	$40.7	$95.8	$130.8	$130.8	$130.8	$528.9
Law Enforcement 3/	$10.0	$15.7	$15.7	$15.7	$15.7	$15.7	$78.5
DEA Support	$4.0	$6.6	$6.6	$6.6	$6.6	$6.6	$33.0
TOTAL	$23.8	$96.7	$159.0	$194.0	$194.0	$194.0	$837.7
TOTAL ASSISTANCE:							
Military Assistance 2	$17.0	$110.5	$141.3	$141.3	$141.3	$141.3	$675.7
Economic Assistance	$5.3	$48.6	$208.9	$283.9	$283.9	$283.9	$1,109.2
Law Enforcement 3/	$30.5	$54.7	$54.7	$54.7	$54.7	$54.7	$273.5
DEA Support	$12.5	$17.8	$17.8	$17.8	$17.8	$17.8	$89.0
GRAND TOTAL	$65.3	$231.6	$422.7	$497.7	$497.7	$497.7	$2,147.4

1/ The obligations projected for FY 1990 are approximate and adjustments may be made during the course of the year. They include Byrd Amendment reductions.

2/ Military assistance includes both Foreign Military Financing (FMF) and International Military Education and Training (IMET). FY 1990 IMET projections are: Colombia, $1.5 million; Peru, $0.5 million; and Bolivia, $0.5 million. FY 1991 IMET projections.are: Colombia, $2.5 million; Peru, $0.9 million; and Bolivia, $0.9 million.

3/ The Law Enforcement category for FY 1990 includes $38.2 million in International Narcotics Matters (INM) funds as well as a portion ($16.5 million) of the $125 million in FMF appropriated for counternarcotics programs in Section 602 of the Foreign Operations, Export Financing, and Related Programs Act for FY 1990.

Office of National Drug Control Policy -- June 20, 1990

Patrol, the Customs Service, the FBI, the Treasury Department, and other agencies are part of anti-narcotics efforts in Andean countries.

The administration's strategy also diverges from previous policy by increasing U.S. economic support to the Andean region on an unprecedented scale.[13] Projected economic assistance for the five-year Andean Initiative totals $203 million for Colombia, $376 million for Peru, and $529 million for Bolivia. The aid is reportedly intended to go to balance of payments support and export promotion, crop substitution and other alternative development activities, drug awareness, and administration of justice programs. In addition, the administration has diversified beyond merely targeting crops through eradication programs, emphasizing targets "higher up" the trafficking chain, such as those who oversee the processing, trafficking, and distribution networks. This shift is an important one, since the cost of eradication falls mostly on peasant producers seeking a livelihood.

While the Andean strategy has sparked increased U.S. pressures on the Andean countries, it has also marked a new emphasis on multi-lateralism in anti-narcotics policy. Although the Andean Initiative was drafted and announced by the United States without input from Andean governments, the administration has viewed Andean governmental cooperation as necessary for any successful source-country efforts. In the face of Andean governments' resistance to unilateral U.S. anti-narcotics plans -- and especially their strong preference for economic assistance and trade benefits over any military aid -- President Bush met with the presidents of Peru, Bolivia and Colombia in Cartagena, Colombia, in February 1990. There a multilateral umbrella accord on anti-narcotics efforts was signed. In the Declaration of Cartagena, the U.S. conceded that it held some responsibility for taking action to curb demand, and, according to a senior administration official, "for the first time" acknowledged that economic support must be provided "to compensate for the loss of coca revenues and to spur economic development."[14] For their part, Andean governments agreed to take "actions against drug trafficking," to undertake "sound economic policies," and to maintain "respect for human rights."[15]

---

[13] Although the Alliance for Progress resulted in comparable amounts of economic assistance, the Andean strategy's five-year total for all three countries is unmatched in the post-war period. Larry Storrs, Congressional Research Service Report 87-694F, July 31, 1987.

[14] Quoted in George de Lama, "Latin Allies Prefer U.S. Money to Military in Drug Fight," The Chicago Tribune, February 13, 1990, p. 8.

[15] ONDCP, "The Andean Strategy," August 1990.

II. THE MILITARY COMPONENT OF THE ANDEAN STRATEGY

Perhaps the Bush administration's most salient break with past approaches is its emphasis on use of military forces in the drug war. The Andean strategy marked the increased use of military forces in two ways:

[1] The Andean strategy called for a systematic increase in U.S. military involvement in source-countries. In announcing the Andean Initiative on September 5, 1989, President Bush said, "The rules have changed.... When requested, we will for the first time make available the appropriate resources of America's armed forces." Two weeks later, Secretary of Defense Richard Cheney upgraded the counter-narcotics mission to a "high priority national security mission" for the Pentagon. He directed all commanders to "elevate the priority of the counter-narcotics mission within your command" and ordered four key commands to submit proposals for anti-narcotics activities by October 15, 1989.

[2] For the first time, U.S. anti-narcotics policy declared Andean armed forces essential to source-country efforts. Assistant Secretary of State for International Narcotics Matters, Melvyn Levitsky, said in June 1990, "Based on our assessment of the situation, we believe that in order to perform, particularly in places like the Upper Huallaga Valley in Peru and in Colombia, the Andean countries need to employ their armed forces as part of the drug war."[16]

A Military Approach vs. An Economic Approach

Despite the administration's claims that its policy is multilateral and multi-faceted, Andean governments have criticized, to varying degrees, the Andean strategy as unduly emphasizing military involvement. According to one U.S. Representative, the ambassadors of all three Andean countries "asked the United States not to provide this level of military assistance,"[17] and Colombia's ambassador to the United States, Víctor Mosquera Chaux, said, "We don't want your troops, ships or planes. But without your economic assistance we could face a reversal of public attitudes in our country toward the struggle against narcotics traffickers."[18] Presidents Jaime Paz Zamora of Bolivia and Alberto Fujimori of Peru have publicly resisted the military

---

[16] Testimony before the House Foreign Affairs Committee, "The Andean Initiative," June 6 and 20, 1990, p. 108. See also U.S. Departments of Defense and State, "Andean Anti-Drug Efforts: A Report to the Congress," issued in compliance with Section 1009 of the Defense Authorization Act for FY 1991, February 1991, p. 2.

[17] Representative Peter Kostmayer, in hearings before the House Foreign Affairs Committee, "The Andean Initiative," June 1990.

[18] Quoted in George de Lama, op cit.

component of the Andean strategy, calling instead for a fundamentally economic approach to the problem.

There is evidence to support their claims. The first three goals of the Andean strategy -- initially the only goals -- focused exclusively on military and law enforcement efforts. The fourth goal of the strategy, "To strengthen and diversify the legitimate economies of the Andean nations to enable them to overcome the destabilizing effects of eliminating cocaine," is the only goal to address economic questions and was added only in 1990, after the Cartagena summit.[19] The administration offered no economic assistance in the first year of the Andean Initiative. Instead, economic aid would be introduced only after military assistance had begun:

> During the first year of the five-year program, it is our intention to provide law enforcement and military assistance to help stabilize the cocaine situation in Peru and Bolivia," said one State Department official.[20]

The administration's goals, formulated without Andean input, imply that the military and law enforcement components of the Andean strategy would play the primary role in "eliminating cocaine" and that economic assistance would subsequently serve to "overcome the destabilizing effects," rather than acting as a catalyst in curbing cocaine production.

After congressional action and talks with Andean officials, the first year of the Andean Initiative (FY 1990) included economic assistance (see table 1.B). However, economic aid totalled only $48 million, compared to a proposed $165 million in military and law enforcement assistance for the three countries. Almost all of the economic assistance went to Bolivia. Although the Andean strategy did not detail the use of economic aid, of the economic assistance requested most recently by the administration for FY 1992, over 88% was for Economic Support Funds (ESF).[21] Over 85% of these ESF funds are slated to go to balance of payments support, rather than development projects. The administration requested only $22.5 million for Bolivia and $15.7 million for Peru in development assistance, a decrease from FY 1990 levels for both countries.

---

[19] See National Drug Control Strateg[ies], September 1989, September 1990.

[20] Parker Borg, Deputy Assistant Secretary of State for International Narcotics Matters, in testimony before the Subcommittee on Legislation and National Security, the Subcommittee on Government Information, Justice and Agriculture, and the House Committee of Government Operations, Oct. 17, 1989.

[21] See Table 4.A, Ch. 4, "Narcotics-Related U.S. Assistance to the Andes," from the House Foreign Affairs Committee.

The administration has acknowledged that a central purpose of U.S. economic assistance to the Andes is to have a lever to get Andean militaries involved in the drug war. Although U.S. officials are careful not to condition economic aid explicitly on acceptance of military aid, the State Department itself has stated (a) that economic assistance is to be withheld as an incentive to elicit Andean nations' cooperation, and (b) that Andean "cooperation" is defined by the involvement of their armed forces and acceptance of U.S. military aid:

> Depending on the successes in the FY 1990 programs, economic assistance might be made available to Peru and Bolivia in FY 1991 to offset some of the negative economic effects of successful cocaine control... It is also our intention to offer this economic assistance as an incentive, which will kick in after we've had a chance to evaluate their use of the augmented law enforcement and military assistance projected for fiscal year 1990."[22]

More recently, the State Department's top anti-drug official responded in congressional hearings to a question about militarization in Bolivia as follows:

> MR. LEVITSKY: Let me be very precise on this, because we have not linked economic assistance to the provision of military assistance.
>
> What we have linked it to is counter-narcotics performance, so if they could do the job without the military, and could perform up to a standard that would allow the keying in of economic assistance, that would be fine.
>
> Our assessment of this is that given the task and the huge distances involved and our experience thus far where they have gotten better but where the situation could be improved, **they could not do it without some infusion of armed forces support for this effort.**"[23]

By including economic elements, the Bush administration has exhibited sensitivity to official Andean views but appears not to have changed its basic belief in the priority of the military component.

---

[22] Deputy Assistant Secretary of State for International Narcotics Matters Parker Borg, testimony, Oct. 17, 1989, op cit.

[23] Assistant Secretary of State for International Narcotics Matters Melvyn Levitsky, "The Andean Initiative," hearings before the House Foreign Affairs Committee, June 6 and 20, 1990, p. 139, emphasis added.

III. THE POLITICS OF MILITARIZATION

The Andean strategy is not grounded in realities in the region, but rather in politics in the United States. Those politics, which respond to very real problems of drug abuse and drug-related violence, are visible in (a) the media and the general public, (b) the Congress, and (c) the Executive branch.

A. Domestic Politics and Militarization

Over the past decade, the serious social situation of drug abuse and drug-related crime and violence has worsened significantly. Over half of felony assaults by young people in 1989 involved drug users, and hospital admissions involving smoked cocaine increased 28-fold between 1984 and 1989.[24] The emergence of the highly addictive cocaine derivative, "crack," in the mid-1980s increased concerns about drug addiction.[25]

In the 1980s increased media attention and calls by domestic constituents for tough action, especially against foreign drug traffickers, created pressures even for members of Congress less inclined toward military action. The following is an excerpt from a local news article on a public forum in New Bedford, Massachusetts, attended by Senators Claiborne Pell (D-RI) and John Kerry (D-MA):

> 'We're not being invaded by Russia,' [New Bedford Mayor John] Bullard said. 'We are daily in New Bedford being invaded by foreign people carrying foreign drugs. Take this message back from New Bedford: We want Washington to stop talking about a war on drugs and start fighting it like you really mean it.'
>
> One after another, local officials said they needed more of everything: more treatment and education programs, more police and special agents, more prison guards and prison cells.
>
> But more than anything else, they said, the federal government must make a moral commitment to go all out in its campaign against international drug cartels.[26]

---

[24] ONDCP, National Drug Control Strategy, September 1989, pp. 1-3.

[25] As of early 1988, polls showed that a majority of Americans considered drugs to be the country's top domestic policy issue, and nearly half of those polled considered drug trafficking to be the United States' #1 international problem (The New York Times, April 10, 1988). By mid-1989, over half of Americans polled favored sending U.S. troops abroad to combat drug traffickers, even though most believed that the traffickers would try to retaliate (Gallup poll for Newsweek, cited in "53% Would Send U.S. Troops to Foreign Drug Fight, Poll Finds," The Baltimore Evening Sun, August 28, 1989, p. 6).

[26] Linda Borg, "Pell says he's willing to send in U.S. troops," Providence Journal-Bulletin, August 30, 1989, p. 1.

B. Congress: Legislating a Wider U.S. Military Role

Throughout the 1980s, Congress became more strident in calls for military involvement. Many members of Congress drew on the language of the "war" on drugs to demand a greater role for the military: "When you have a war, who do you call in to fight the war? You call the military in."[27] In the face of what they perceived as foot-dragging on the part of the Department of Defense, some representatives strongly criticized the military. These criticisms included calls for action against drug cartels, but centered on the military's role in domestic support efforts and in border interdiction. One of the leaders in legislating an expanded role for the military, Rep. Nicholas Mavroules (D-MA), said that Congress had been "met at every turn by determined opposition from the Department of Defense."[28] Congressional support for military involvement spanned the political spectrum, as neither party wanted to appear "soft" on drugs.

Through legislation, Congress played an important role in steadily widening the U.S. military's role in the drug war. In 1981, Congress amended the Posse Comitatus Act, which since 1878 has restricted U.S. armed forces personnel from participating in law enforcement activities. The changes allowed the military to provide equipment, information, training, and advice to law enforcement agencies. The amendment retained the prohibition on military participation in search, seizure, and arrests, but permitted assistance to foreign law enforcement agencies if certain "emergency circumstances" exist.[29]

Despite the expanded use of the U.S. military, Congress was increasingly frustrated at the lack of progress in the drug war. Cocaine production continued to climb through the end of the decade. Congress increased federal spending for demand and supply reduction programs in the Anti-Drug Abuse Acts of 1986 and 1988.[30] In addition to a series of stronger law enforcement measures against drug-related offenses, the 1986 Act enacted an annual suspension of 50% of all foreign aid to drug producing and drug transit countries unless the President "certifies" each year that those countries are

---

[27] Representative Jack Davis (R-IL).

[28] See hearings before Mavroules' Investigations Subcommittee, House Armed Services Committee, "Military Role in Drug Interdiction," February 22, 1989, p. 2.

[29] Also in 1981, Representative Clay Shaw introduced an amendment which would allow direct military participation in seizures and arrest outside U.S. territory. The Defense Department teamed up with civil libertarians and the criminal defense bar to help defeat passage of the proposal, arguing that it would be a raid on military resources.

[30] Bruce Bagley, "The Myth of Militarization: An Evaluation of the Role of the Military in the War on Drugs in the Americas," in Proceedings: "Latin America Strategy Development Workshop," 26-27 September, 1990, at the National Defense University, p. 97.

fully cooperating with U.S. anti-drug efforts.[31] If a country is not certified or is not taking steps on its own, then the U.S. Executive Directors of the various multilateral development banks (including the World Bank, the International Development Agency, and the Inter-American Development Bank) must vote against all loans to that country. In egregious cases, the U.S. might withhold all aid. During the presidential and congressional campaign of 1988, when drugs became a leading issue, the second major Anti-Drug Abuse Act was passed by Congress which toughened the sanctions against countries not meeting the "certification" requirements, authorized certain military assistance funding for Latin American anti-narcotics efforts, and loosened the constraints on U.S. aid to foreign police forces.[32]

Still frustrated, the House of Representatives in 1988 passed a bill which would have required the U.S. military to seal U.S. borders within 45 days, given the military arrest powers, and authorized hot pursuit of suspected drug smugglers into foreign territory.[33] Senate leaders, including Sen. Sam Nunn (D-GA), moved to head off the extreme proposal and reached a compromise.[34] The Defense Authorization Act for FY 1989 (1) made the Department of Defense (DOD) the single lead agency for the detection and monitoring of aerial and maritime transit of illegal drugs into the United States, (2) required DOD to integrate the communications and technical intelligence assets of the various federal agencies into a single network, and (3) required DOD to coordinate the increased us of the National Guard in anti-narcotics activities.

Finally, concern was voiced within Congress as to the ineffectiveness of, and the dangers posed by, paramilitary U.S. law enforcement programs in the Andes. In March of 1987, the DEA initiated "Operation Snowcap," which introduced temporary (90-day) agents into Bolivia, Peru and Ecuador, to help plan, advise, and coordinate anti-drug raids on cocaine processing laboratories, clandestine airstrips, and the various stages of cocaine trafficking. Following investigative missions, Operation Snowcap was severely criticized because DEA agents were deemed insufficiently prepared either to combat heavily armed trafficking organizations or to enter coca-growing regions in Peru where the Sendero Luminoso (Shining Path) guerrillas are active.[35] A House

---

[31] Harry Hogan, et al, "Drug Control: Highlights of PL99-570, Anti-Drug Abuse Act of 1986," Congressional Research Service document 86-968 GOV, October 31, 1986.

[32] See Anti-Drug Abuse Act of 1988, and Raphael Perl, "Congress, International Narcotics Control Policy, and the Anti-Drug Abuse Act of 1988," in Journal of Inter-American Studies and World Affairs, Vol. 30, Summer/Fall 1988.

[33] See "Flak Hits Troop Role in Drug War," Insight, The Washington Times, June 20, 1988, p. 22.

[34] Personal interviews with a Senate staff member involved in discussions between Senate conferees and the administration.

[35] House Committee on Foreign Affairs, Report of a Staff Study Mission, "U.S. Narcotics Control Programs in Peru, Bolivia, Colombia and Mexico: An Update," February 1989, p. 4.

Foreign Affairs Committee staff report stated in 1989 that the DEA was inappropriate for jungle operations and urged the executive branch to consider the use of U.S. Special Forces.[36] Many in the administration shared the concerns over the security of U.S. DEA agents.

C. The Bush Administration and "Going to the Source"

The Reagan administration incrementally expanded military participation, but was criticized by Congress and the media for not doing more. In April 1986, President Reagan signed National Security Decision Directive #221 declaring drug trafficking a threat to the national security of the United States. Under his administration overall federal spending increased steadily, including the military's anti-drug budget, which grew from less than $5 million in 1982 to over $200 million in FY 1988.[37]

Throughout the Reagan years, however, the Defense Department did no strategic planning of anti-narcotics operations but simply responded to calls from U.S. law enforcement agencies, both at home and abroad. In the Andes, the military role consisted of providing transportation for police and (later) limited assistance in training. Between July and November of 1986, for example, 160 U.S. Army troops and six helicopters were used to transport Bolivian anti-narcotics police and DEA agents to raid processing labs in that country. It was the first U.S. military operation in support of counter-narcotics activities in the Andes.[38] Operation Snowcap initiated the following year was the immediate antecedent to the Andean strategy. In addition to DEA agents and elements of the State Department, the U.S. Coast Guard, and the Border patrol, Operation Snowcap initiated continuous rotations of teams of U.S. Army Special Forces ("Green Berets") who train Andean police units.

As a presidential candidate, George Bush indicated that he would assign a higher profile to international anti-narcotics efforts. During the 1988 campaign, he distanced himself from the Reagan administration's position by advocating a shift in focus from border interdiction to "source-country" efforts.[39] In doing so he demonstrated an early responsiveness to the concerns of the foreign policy bureaucracy. The Departments of State and Defense and

---

[36] Ibid.

[37] Figures from Bagley, op cit., p. 91., and from National Drug Control Strategy, September 1989, Appendix B.

[38] Portending opposition to the Andean strategy six years later, the use of the troops sparked a sharp nationalist outcry in Bolivia. In an interview with WOLA, one State Department official called the operation a "diplomatic disaster."

[39] George Bush, quoted in David Hoffman, "Halt Drugs at the Source, Suggests Bush," The Washington Post, May 27, 1988.

the DEA all supported a shift away from border interdiction to source-country programs.[40]   Then-Assistant Secretary of State for International Narcotics Matters Ann Wrobleski said, "I would argue that, if you took all the money that we are going to spend to ring the southern border with hardware and spend it in the Andes in military assistance as well as in development and economic support..., it is a wiser use of the taxpayers' dollar."[41]   Admiral Frank Kelso, Commander-in-Chief of the U.S. Atlantic Fleet, echoed those sentiments before Congress:

> "Interdiction is the most difficult and most expensive initiative to fight drugs. In military terms, it is like attempting to shoot down the missile after it is fired rather than hitting the shooter. We must shoot the archer, not the arrow!"[42]

Upon taking office in 1989, Bush began to lay the legal groundwork for increased military action in the drug war abroad.[43]   In August, Bush signed National Security Directive 18, authorizing armed forces personnel to go beyond "secure areas" in narcotics-related programs abroad, essentially permitting troops to go into areas of potential conflict with guerrillas or traffickers.[44]   In November, the U.S. Department of Justice office of legal counsel issued a legal opinion that U.S. military personnel could arrest foreign citizens in other countries -- a power that the Posse Comitatus Act denies the

---

[40] Ann Wrobleski, Assistant Secretary for International Narcotics Matters, U.S. State Department, in Seminar held May 8, 1987, for the Senate Caucus on International Narcotics Control, "Combatting International Drug Cartels: Issues for U.S. Policy," pp. 29-31. Also, see statement of Terrence M. Burke, then Acting Deputy Administrator, DEA, in hearings before the House Foreign Affairs Committee, "Review of President's Andean Initiative," p. 15. Also, remarks of Lt. Gen. Stephen Olmstead, DOD Drug Policy Coordinator, Proceedings of a seminar...., op cit., p. 24, and testimony of former SOUTHCOM commander Paul Gorman, hearings before Senate Committee on Foreign Relations, "Drugs, Law Enforcement, and Foreign Policy: Panama," February 8, 1988, pp. 33-36.

[41] Ibid.

[42] Testimony of Secretary of Defense Frank Carlucci and Admiral Frank Kelso, before the Senate Armed Services Committee, June 15, 1988.

[43] Personnel changes also marked the shift. Bush's own experience as head of the South Florida Task Force when he was Vice-President may have contributed to a frustration with border interdiction efforts.   Secretary Cheney's commitment of the U.S. military to "enthusiastic participation" in the drug war stands in stark contrast to the stance of his predecessors Frank Carlucci and Caspar Weinberger. And in mid-1989, two Army generals were nominated by President Bush for what would be key posts in the war on drugs. Gen. Colin Powell, named to head the Joint Chiefs of Staff, also distinguished himself from his predecessors by pledging in his confirmation hearings to fully support a greater engagement of the armed forces in countering drug trafficking (See Richard Halloran, "Gen. Powell Sees Risk if Military Enters Drug War," The New York Times, September 21, 1989. Powell acknowledged that the role would entail risks, but said "it's a risk worth taking"). Gen. Maxwell Thurman, brought out of retirement to head SouthCom, became the military's most renowned drug warrior after ousting Gen. Noriega from Panama. Both Powell and Thurman took command on October 1, 1989.

[44] George C. Wilson and Michael Isikoff, "U.S. Advisers Allowed to Leave Latin Bases," The Washington Post, Sept. 13, 1989.

military in United States territory.[45]   In addition, the Judge Advocate General's office of the Army, with the concurrence of the other military departments, the State Department and the CIA, concluded in a draft memorandum that the use of "military force against a terrorist or terrorist organization is a legitimate exercise of the international legal right of self defense and does not constitute assassination."[46] And in early 1990, officials of the U.S. Special Operations Command announced that they were seeking exemption from classified pre-operation review processes in order to act with more freedom from the oversight of administrative and congressional bodies.[47]

The concepts underlying the Andean strategy were, therefore, in place well before the strategy was announced.   Indeed, while the Bush administration initiated the widening of both the U.S. and the Andean militaries' role in source-country efforts, the policy responds to domestic political pressures which date back at least to President Reagan's first term. Neither Andean governments nor other groups in the region were consulted in drafting the plan. Ultimately, the domestic push for action against drugs is critical to understanding the motives, the prospects for success, and the dangers of the military component of the Andean strategy.

---

[45] Michael Isikoff and Patrick Tyler, "U.S. Military Given Foreign Arrest Power," The Washington Post, December 16, 1989. In February 1990, the U.S. Supreme Court ruled that U.S. law enforcement agents could conduct searches and seizures abroad without the search warrant required for domestic searches and seizures under the Fourth Amendment. See "Justices Uphold Property Searches of Foreigners in Foreign Countries," The New York Times, March 1, 1990.

[46] Copy of Draft Memorandum, DAJA-IA(27-1A), by Maj. Gen. Hugh R. Overholt, Judge Advocate General, USA, undated, released April 17, 1989.

[47] See Molly Moore, "Senators Say Military Easing Reins on Special Forces," The Washington Post, May 23, 1990; and John Broder and Melissa Healy, "Military Fights for Freer Role in Covert Operations," The Los Angeles Times, April 6, 1990.

CHAPTER 2

THE U.S. MILITARY AND THE ANDEAN STRATEGY

Chapter Summary

The role of the U.S. military has been among the most controversial aspects of the war on drugs. The White House and the Pentagon, committed to avoiding "another Vietnam," have settled on a strategy that sets limits on the role of U.S. military forces. U.S. military personnel are not permitted to engage in actual combat, and the strategy does not require large numbers of U.S. troops. Tentative proposals to send Marines to the Andes or to conduct aerial strikes in support of multi-national attacks on trafficker targets have not been accepted. While military officials and analysts acknowledge that U.S. involvement could evolve in unforeseen ways, especially in Peru, the administration has consistently disclaimed any intentions beyond operational support for U.S. and Andean law enforcement efforts. Accordingly, the military component of the Andean strategy depends critically upon the participation of Andean armed forces and draws on U.S. security assistance programs as the chief instrument of the policy.

Given those parameters, the U.S. military involvement in the drug war in the Andes is expanding sharply. The administration has approved plans, drafted by the U.S. Southern Command (SouthCom), for a host of new drug-related activities in the Andes. In recognition of the increasingly diffuse and flexible cocaine trade, the plans foresee expanded U.S. military operational support for security forces in Central America and the rest of South America. The plans draw heavily on recent technology for intelligence-gathering equipment. They aim to increase Latin American intelligence-gathering capabilities, to train Andean militaries and police forces in an array of tasks, and to provide millions of dollars worth of equipment to those forces. In Bolivia and Peru the plan calls for small teams of U.S. military specialists to select targets, plan raids, and coordinate operations carried out by the DEA and Andean police and military forces. And reports of a U.S. military role in the aerial raid that killed drug leader Gonzalo Rodríguez Gacha indicate that those plans may include involvement in covert operations. The Central Intelligence Agency (CIA) says that it is devoting one-fourth of its resources in Latin America to the drug war, and is playing a central role in inter-agency intelligence activities related to international anti-narcotics efforts.

For the U.S. military, the anti-narcotics mission has mobilized institutional resources and strategies which will have implications for several years and which are being applied throughout the Latin American region. While the Department of Defense has staunchly opposed expanded roles in border interdiction and in anti-narcotics activities within the United States, the

U.S. Southern Command and other entities within the Pentagon have enthusiastically embraced the drug war. Military officials acknowledge that the counter-narcotics mission serves important interests of the U.S. military in Latin America at a critical time. It gives the military a new mission in the hemisphere just as the Cold War has changed the nature of U.S. military strategy worldwide. It also converges with new post-Cold War opportunities to strengthen bilateral relations with the armed forces of Latin America. And, unlike new anti-drug roles on the domestic side such as logistical support for law enforcement agencies and border interdiction (which the military has resisted as detracting from its central mission), it converges with previous low-intensity conflict roles in Latin America. These institutional developments indicate that the military component of the drug war is unlikely to be a quick, surgical operation serving as a preliminary stage to social and economic programs, but a multi-year effort that military officials will apply to other countries in the hemisphere.

I. SETTING THE LIMITS: U.S. TROOP AUTHORIZATION IN THE ANDES

The intense level of alarm in the U.S. over cocaine-related problems in the late 1980s -- resulting in, and fed by, U.S. media led to calls that troops be sent into combat in the Andes. In Congress, some of these calls were general bids for sending troops without much detail about what the troops would actually do. In August 1989, following the assassination of Colombian presidential candidate Luis Carlos Galán, then-Attorney General Richard Thornburgh said that the U.S. would consider sending U.S. troops to Colombia.[1] The comments, which came on the heels of Bush's decision to widen the operational flexibility of U.S. troops in the Andes, sparked widespread debate in the U.S. media over the role of U.S. troops in the Andes.[2] In September 1989, top Pentagon sources said they were drawing up plans for U.S. Marines to enter into operations against drug traffickers' bases in conjunction with Latin American forces.[3]

However, the Bush administration has consistently rejected any direct combat role for U.S. troops like that in Grenada, Panama, or Vietnam. Following Thornburgh's statement, President Bush quickly said that the

---

[1] Some in the press corps viewed Thornburgh's remarks as airing a trial balloon for the public. Ethan Bronner, "US aide talks of troop help for Colombia," The Baltimore Sun, August 21, 1989, p. 1; R.W. Apple, "The Capital," The New York Times, August 23, 1989, p. 18.

[2] See editorials and articles reproduced in the Department of Defense's "Current News: Special Edition" on the Military Role in the Drug War, No. 1807, October 18, 1989.

[3] Peter Almond, "Marines Enlisted in Drug War, May Help Raid Bases," The Washington Times, September 21, 1989, p. 3.

proposal was not under serious consideration.[4] Since then the administration has steadily maintained that U.S. troops will not engage in direct combat: "...nor do we contemplate sending U.S. military forces into the jungles of the Andes to fight the drug war."[5]

The administration has also demonstrated some awareness that its influence in the more complex and distant societies of the Andes is not comparable to its influence in Central America. Some tentative proposals involving conventional military operations aired by the administration have been postponed or shelved in the face of opposition from Andean governments. In January of 1990, two weeks after the invasion of Panama, top Pentagon officials leaked a proposal of a "virtual air and sea blockade" of all drugs flowing out of Colombia, and the Navy subsequently dispatched the first ships of an air carrier group.[6] In response to a public outcry in Colombia, President Bush promptly ordered the first ships of the carrier group into port and assured Colombian President Virgilio Barco that no such action would be taken without his consent.[7] A few months later SouthCom leaked a proposal (without the Pentagon's approval) of U.S.-planned and U.S.-coordinated simultaneous air and ground assaults, to be conducted by Andean forces, against the major trafficking sites in Colombia, Bolivia and Peru.[8] In this case, the plan drew sharp criticism from the Bolivian government and was quickly disavowed by the Pentagon.[9]

The announcement in August 1991 that over 50 U.S. trainers would be sent to advise the Peruvian armed forces in anti-narcotics and counter-insurgency rekindled concerns in the U.S. press about a direct combat role for U.S. troops.[10] SouthCom officials and military analysts acknowledge that there

---

[4] Ibid.

[5] Assistant Secretary of State for International Narcotics Matters Melvyn Levitsky, "Review of the 1991 International Narcotics Control Strategy Report," House Foreign Affairs Committee, (hereafter "Review of the 1991 INCSR"), March 5, 1991, p. 22. This is only one example of many.

[6] Stan Yarbro and Susanne M. Schafer, "Pentagon Wants to Use Air, Sea to Fight Colombian Drug Trade," Ft. Worth Star-Telegram, Dec. 28, 1990. Also John Broder, "Two U.S. Warships Sailing to Colombia for Drug Patrol," The Los Angeles Times, January 7, 1990.

[7] "U.S. Denies it has plans to 'blockade' Colombia," The Baltimore Sun, Jan. 9, 1990; "U.S. Postpones Deploying Ships Near Colombia," The New York Times, January 17, 1990.

[8] Douglas Waller et al, "Risky Business," Newsweek, July 16, 1990. One SouthCom official reported to WOLA that the proposal even included sending U.S. planes from Howard Air Force Base in Panama to bomb selected sites. Personal interviews in early 1991.

[9] See Pentagon press conference, July 9, 1990. SouthCom officers report that the plan is on the shelf, but that the command would be eager to activate it if the Andean governments so requested.

[10] For example, The New York Times columnist Tom Wicker explicitly compared the situation to Vietnam and El Salvador: "...officials add, of course, that U.S. troops...will be 'trainers' only, as they originally were in Vietnam and as they have been for years in El Salvador." See "The Peru Syndrome," Aug. 8, 1991.

are some "gung-ho" officers who would welcome a direct combat role and that involvement in counter-insurgency support in Peru may lead to unforeseen involvement on a deeper level.[11]   A direct combat role for U.S. troops continues to have proponents, although they are a small minority in the military.   In February 1991, Col. Robert Jacobelly, the commander of all U.S. Special Forces in Central and South America, responded as follows to the question, "Will U.S. troops get directly involved in operations in the field?":

> It depends a lot on Desert Storm.   I think that [if Desert Storm is successful] things are going to change, and we'll be told, "Go get 'em."   And my guys will be very happy.[12]

According to one specialist on U.S. anti-narcotics policy, military analysts themselves recognize the volatility of even a U.S. support role:

> [U.S.] military planners are determined not to let [a Vietnam-type jungle war] scenario develop.   Nevertheless, analysts warn that, once shooting starts, it would be difficult to disengage from the conflict, particularly if there is strong initial pressure from home to respond. In addition, there is general agreement that, as counter-narcotics programs increase in effectiveness, so does the likelihood of US military casualties from traffickers and insurgents alike."[13]

To date the evidence indicates that "another Vietnam" -- i.e., the involvement of large numbers of U.S. troops in direct operations -- is not at hand.   The administration remains committed to limiting the number of troops in the region to several hundred and to restricting overt military activities to support roles, not operations.[14]   Whatever the broad effect of the Gulf War on the administration's propensity to resort to military force, there is no evidence that that war or any other factors have shifted these limitations.   The administration has not changed the tone of its public statements on the U.S. military role.[15]   In addition, the urgency of demands within the U.S. Congress and the press for forceful action has subsided, and the administration has

---

[11] Interviews with two SouthCom officials, early 1991, and with civilian analysts familiar with the Pentagon, mid-1991.

[12] Interview with Col. Robert Jacobelly, head of Special Operations Command South (SOCSOUTH), and commander of all U.S. Special Forces in Central and South America. Quarry Heights, Panama, February 15, 1991.

[13] Raphael Perl, Specialist in International Affairs, Congressional Research Service, "U.S. International Drug Policy: Recent Developments and Issues," Journal of Inter-American Studies and World Affairs, Vol. 32, No. 4, Winter 1990, pp. 131-132.

[14] The possibility of covert operations, as illustrated by the Newsday story, remains open.

[15] See, e.g., the statement earlier in this section by Assistant Secretary Levitsky from March 1991.

increasingly recognized the need for cooperation from Andean governments, who remain opposed to any direct, overt U.S. military combat role.

II. THE PENTAGON'S ANTI-DRUG PLAN

Within the parameters set by the White House, the Pentagon has launched a massive multi-year anti-narcotics strategy for Latin America. On March 9, 1990, the Pentagon announced that the administration had approved in final form the plans submitted by the five relevant commanders in response to Secretary Cheney's directive in September 1989. The Southern Command "campaign plan" was described as including all manner of operational support to host countries. Col. Larry Izzo, of the Operations Directorate of the Joint Staff, said that "Operational support is defined as any manner of support to host nation operations short of actually participating in those operations." In describing the campaign plan, Col. Izzo said:

> "We will assist the host nations in developing the capacity to control their own air corridors...

> "We will also increase the capacity of the countries to conduct operations on their rivers by providing them patrol boats, again through security assistance programs, and by helping train their forces on river operations. We will assist with the flow of tactical information into the region. We will also try to help the host nations develop their own capacity to collect and disseminate intelligence, and we'll try to provide intelligence from our own national and theater assets to the host nations through the embassies.

> "We will also train both their military forces as well as their police forces, again using security assistance funds. We will improve their air mobile capabilities by providing helicopters and training them on air mobile operations. We'll also assist in training them on joint military and police operations."[16]

According to Izzo, SouthCom's anti-drug program had a budget of $230 million in FY 1990 and $430 million in FY 1991.

SouthCom strategy documents show that the anti-drug plan for Latin America centers on the Andes, but extends to Central America and the rest of South America. The command divides the region into three "tiers":

---

[16] Remarks, Department of Defense News Briefing, Friday, March 9, 1990.

Tier I: Colombia, Peru and Bolivia
Tier II: Ecuador, Venezuela, Brazil and the Southern Cone
Tier III: Central America and Panama.[17]

For fiscal years 1990 and 1991, SouthCom's priorities are the Tier I countries where the goal of Phase #1 is to "seize the initiative". In FY 1992, the command plans to initiate Phase #2 in the Andean ridge, aimed at assisting "host nations to take [the] offensive." It will also devote more resources to Tiers II and III, beginning to implement security assistance programs similar to those undertaken in the Andes. During Phase #3 of its campaign, slated for "outyears" after FY 1992, SouthCom intends to consolidate its efforts, leaving host nations "self-sufficient". SouthCom planners state that they see the drug mission as a priority for the next five to seven years.[18] Similarly, the DEA plans to replicate its Operation Snowcap in other countries in the hemisphere, and the State Department is making the drug war a higher priority for the rest of the hemisphere.[19]

High-tech intelligence equipment plays a key part in the Pentagon's plan. SouthCom is in the process of expanding a pilot program of a complex $143-million intelligence network, called the Command Management System. The system will rely on satellites and tactical radar to link up DEA and Andean police agents in the field to that country's embassy, to SouthCom's Counter-narcotics Center in Panama, and ultimately to a series of intelligence coordination centers in the United States.[20] Feeding into the Command Management System is a series of eighteen radar -- some already in place in the Caribbean, the Andes and Central America, and some not yet operational -- called the Caribbean Basin Radar Network. The system aims to enable U.S. agents to transmit a photograph or other data to the United States and receive information back in a matter of minutes. In the past such intelligence communication has taken days as the raw data had to be carried back and forth to the United States by aircraft.[21] Other intelligence activities involve AWACS and E-2C Hawkeye radar aircraft, reconnaissance planes, and U.S.

---

[17] The information on the plans for the three "tiers" and the phases for those plans are from SouthCom strategy documents, October 1990; personal interviews with SouthCom officials, early 1991.

[18] Interviews with Col. Carson and Lt. Col. Tim McMahon, J-5, Policy and Planning, Quarry Heights, Panama, early 1991.

[19] Interview with Charles Gutensohn, then-Chief, Cocaine Investigations Section, DEA, February 1991.

[20] The link-up involves satellite hook-ups and a series of tactical radars placed in eighteen sites throughout the Caribbean Basin region, including Colombia, Venezuela, Panama, Honduras, the Dominican Republic, Cuba and Puerto Rico. SouthCom Strategy documents, October 1990.

[21] SouthCom strategy documents, October 1990, slide 5-11.

Navy ships offshore.[22] Ground sensors which detect movement are to be used on pathways trod by traffickers.

Of more direct significance for Latin America are the Pentagon's plans to upgrade the capabilities of intelligence branches within police and military forces in the region. Just as U.S. agencies have moved toward centralizing and integrating all U.S. drug-related intelligence systems in the past three years, military officials view the centralization and improvement of Andean intelligence operations and networks critical to success in the drug war. For example, the bilateral Bolivian-U.S. anti-drug accord signed in May 1990 includes the centralization of military and police intelligence. SouthCom documents deem "intelligence fusion" and "data fusion" -- the timely and effective coordination of information -- important to overall efforts.[23]

Although the Pentagon's plans depend ultimately on Andean police and military forces to carry out the operations in those countries, with U.S. forces providing only support, neither Andean civilian leaders, Andean law enforcement officials nor Andean military officials were initially consulted about the training program designed for their security forces. In 1989-90, SouthCom developed, in conjunction with the Army/Air Force Center for Low Intensity Conflict (CLIC), what an internal DEA document describes as an "integrated training strategy for host country forces conducting counter-narcotics operations." The document describes the training proposal as follows:

> "Under the generic plan now available, each country will provide for training six military strike battalions, their staffs, a police strike company, and a national level military staff. Country specific plans will be based on a survey of the host country needs and capabilities.

> The program will take six months and use the train-the-trainer concept. At that time, each unit should have a trained cadre capable of maintaining training readiness. When the core training is complete,a team of military advisers, with one DEA Special Agent, will remain with each battalion for 18 months, or longer, if necessary. This advisory body is called an Operational Planning Assistance and Training Team (OPATT)...

> Mobile Training Teams (MTT) will provide standardized progressive training to host country personnel. Progressive training

---

[22] See "The Widening Drug War," Newsweek, July 1, 1991.

[23] SouthCom strategy documents, October 1990.

in the United States will also be made available to selected host country officers, commanders, and battalion staff members. The MTT training will include two-week riverine training for selected host country personnel."[24]

The initial draft of the plan was designed exclusively by U.S. agencies -- especially the CLIC and the DEA -- that drew on prior military training programs given to Operation Snowcap agents.[25] Before the Andean strategy was announced, the U.S. had already trained dozens of Bolivian and Peruvian police agents in support of Operation Snowcap. However, under the new plan all four services -- the U.S. Army, Air Force, Navy and Marines -- will train their counterparts in skills ranging from jungle warfare to psychological operations to riverine patrols and air support skills to communications to the operation and maintenance of U.S.-donated equipment. Civil affairs operations -- such as sending of U.S. engineer and medical units and the training of such units among regional military forces -- have expanded and are increasingly considered part of the counter-narcotics mission.[26]

Part of the Pentagon's law enforcement support role is the planning and coordinating of the military and paramilitary police efforts within hemispheric anti-narcotics efforts. The military has devised "Tactical Analysis Teams (TATs)" which work out of each U.S. embassy to coordinate all intelligence on drug trafficking within the country. These TATs, staffed by military intelligence officers and U.S. Special Forces personnel, plan the details of drug raids conducted by DEA agents and Andean police and armed forces.[27] Although Andean officials are nominally consulted about the content of U.S. military training programs, in practice the training programs have been designed by the Defense Department in the United States and are included in bilateral agreements.[28]

Reports of a U.S. role in the attempted capture of Medellín cartel leader Gonzalo Rodríguez Gacha illustrate how the U.S. military may be working in covert anti-narcotics operations in the Andes. In May 1990, Newsday

---

[24] Drug Enforcement Administration Review, "Institution Building in the Andean Nations," October 26, 1989, reprinted in hearings before the House Foreign Affairs Committee, "Operation Snowcap: Past, Present, and Future," May 23, 1990, p. 55. As noted later, parts of this plan appear to have been abandoned.

[25] Personal interview with a mid-level Army officer who played a key part in drafting the plans for the Center for Low Intensity Conflict, early 1991. The officer requested anonymity.

[26] Personal interview with SouthCom officials. Early 1991 and August 1991.

[27] Interviews with SouthCom and other U.S. government officials. Also "The Widening Drug War," Newsweek, July 1, 1991.

[28] See DEA internal review document, op cit.; also interviews with SouthCom officials and with military officers who designed the training component of the Andean strategy at the Army-Air Force Center for Low-Intensity Conflict, early 1991.

reported that U.S. forces helped plan and lead an air assault in which Rodríguez Gacha had been slain on his ranch in Colombia.[29] The article drew on information provided by a Special Operations officer familiar with the details of the operation, three other Defense Department officials, and a staff member from each of the House and Senate. The Special Operations officer said that the plan was to capture Rodríguez Gacha and credit the Colombians with the capture, although events did not go as planned. The article reported that sources varied somewhat on the extent of the U.S. role, but two confirmed that a U.S. special operations team both planned and directed the raid. Two sources identified the North American team leader as the overall commander of the operation, and a military intelligence source said that Colombian police involved in the operation were "used...almost as window dressing." One congressional source said, "Officially we say they did it, but in fact it was us." According to the article, another source "with close ties to U.S. intelligence" said that,

> ...four Spanish-speaking Americans aboard two U.S.-built Huey helicopters operated the radios and sophisticated electronic equipment linking them to a U.S. satellite tracking the traffickers below. At least one of the helicopters, he said, belonged to the U.S. Southern Command headquartered in Panama. He said the Americans had operational control of the mission and that Colombians manned the M-60 machine guns...[30]

In the article, one source said that one of the North Americans was a U.S. Army officer detached to the CIA for several years, and a second source reported that U.S. military personnel were brought in specifically for the mission. Two congressional staff members said that both the House and Senate intelligence committees were notified of the operation through a presidential "finding" required for any covert operations. President Bush disavowed the involvement of U.S. troops, but a senior administration official stopped short of outright denial: "We were not aware of it here."[31]

The CIA has become increasingly involved in anti-narcotics activities. The Agency has been widely criticized for hindering anti-narcotics efforts by finding allies for the fight against communism among foreign security officials who were involved in the drug trade. In mid-1989, however, the CIA announced it would devote one-fourth of its efforts in Latin America to the

---

[29] The article, written by Knut Royce and Peter Eisner from Newsday's Washington bureau five months after the incident, drew on sources that requested anonymity and were reluctant to discuss any of the details of the operation: "U.S. Got Gacha," Long Island Newsday, May 4, 1990.

[30] This quote, as all the information in this paragraph, is from the Long Island Newsday article, ibid.

[31] Ibid.

drug war, and in 1990 spokesperson James Greenleaf said, "narcotics is a new priority."[32] In January 1990, the CIA's Office of the Inspector General wrote that the CIA's Counter-narcotics Center "is emerging as a focal point for decisions on all [intelligence] activities" -- unsurprising given the CIA's mandate.[33] At the same time, the CIA has long had the capacity and responsibility for covert operations in foreign countries, and these operations have been known to draw on U.S. military personnel. In recent years the U.S. military has enhanced its capacity for covert operations utilizing "special operations forces." In 1987, at Congress' insistence, the Defense Department founded the "U.S. Special Operations Command" to oversee all U.S. special operations forces.[34]   Special Operations Forces increased in number from 19,000 to 38,000 since 1985, and a new Special Forces Group was recently created. Although overall Defense forces are slated for reduction by 25% by 1996, in May 1991 DOD's top Low-Intensity Conflict official said that the budget for Special Operations continues to grow and that two new battalions of Special Forces are planned by 1992.[35]

III. THE INSTITUTIONAL IMPLICATIONS OF TURNING TO THE MILITARY

The implications of turning to the military -- both the U.S. military and the Andean militaries -- have not been fully examined by U.S. policymakers. The involvement of the armed forces in a new policy area, especially one as complex as anti-narcotics policy, has significant institutional implications. Military approaches are oriented toward overcoming all obstacles to accomplish the mission assigned them. And the military approaches problems in a comprehensive manner, planning with a multi-year, global approach. Military officials have been quick to point out that the military's job -- destruction of targets or enemies -- contrasts sharply with the task of law enforcement agencies -- arrests, searches, seizures and the maintenance of public order. Analysts have pointed out that in the drug war, as in counter-insurgency, identifying the enemy in field operations is difficult. Given that Andean forces are tapped for carrying out the mission, their propensity for not sufficiently distinguishing between armed insurgents and unarmed civilians in their counter-insurgency campaigns poses serious questions about military

---

[32] Greenleaf cited in Jeff Gerth, "CIA Shedding its Reluctance to Aid in Fight Against Drugs," The New York Times, March 25, 1990.

[33] Office of the Inspector General of the Department of State, "Inspection of the Bureau of International Narcotics Matters," ISP/I-90-4, January 1990, p. 31.

[34] See Appendix A for more details about Special Operations Forces.

[35] Remarks by Assistant Secretary of Defense for Special Operations and Low Intensity Conflict James R. Locher III, at Conference on "Special Operations, Low Intensity Conflict, and Drug Interdiction," Washington, DC, May 13-14, 1991.

involvement. And, like any institution, when confronted with obstacles to its approach to complex social problems, the military's tendency is likely to be continuation of the plan, making certain adjustments and expanding resources, rather than fundamental questioning of the strategy.

A. The Drug War and the Military's Budgetary Interests

Military officials acknowledge that the drug war serves important institutional interests of the U.S. military in Latin America at a critical time. First, these officials admit that pending cuts in military forces have softened the Pentagon's previous opposition to expanded anti-narcotics activities. Throughout the 1980s, the Department of Defense resisted congressional efforts to get the Pentagon more involved in supporting law enforcement agencies. Former Secretaries of Defense Caspar Weinberger and Frank Carlucci strongly opposed the anti-drug mission. The main objections raised by the Pentagon were concerns that the military would be drawn into law enforcement functions and that counter-drug work would adversely affect the military's preparedness for carrying out its central mission of national defense. In addition, the Pentagon's top drug policy official openly expressed his skepticism about Congress' motives in turning to the military:

> "What I find is, ... 'let's make the Army a scapegoat. We don't know the answer to the drug problem, so let's assign it to the Army and let them try and solve it'."[36]

Military officials consistently told Congress that the answer to America's drug problem lay on the <u>demand</u> side.[37] By ordering the military to "enthusiastically embrace" the drug war, Secretary Cheney stimulated a transformation of the military's public stance. Cheney's guidance of September 1989, was widely viewed as a signal of the White House's resolve to end the Pentagon's rear-guard resistance.[38] Since then, civilian and military leaders within the Department of Defense have publicly displayed a positive attitude about the efforts being made, and are genuinely satisfied that a role in making arrests at home was averted.

---

[36] Lt. Gen. Stephen Olmstead, in "Narcotics Interdiction and the Use of the Military: Issues for Congress," Report on a Seminar held by Congressional Research Service, June 7, 1988, p. 13.

[37] See especially statements by Secretary of Defense Frank Carlucci, III, and by Admiral Frank Kelso, II, in joint hearings before the Senate and House Armed Services Committees, June 15, 1988, p. 5; statements by Lt. Gen. Stephen Olmstead, Deputy Assistant Secretary of Defense for Drug Policy and Enforcement, in proceedings of a seminar held by Congressional Research Service, June 7, 1988, published by the Investigations Subcommittee of the House Armed Services Committee, Aug. 24, 1988, p. 13; and personal interview with Lt. Gen. Stephen Olmstead (ret.), March 1991.

[38] See Doug Jehl and Melissa Healy, "In Reversal, Military Seeks Drug War Role," The Los Angeles Times, Dec. 15, 1989, p. 1.

At the same time, institutional interests have played a part in muting the miitary's opposition to the drug war. The fall of the Berlin wall and the watershed changes in Eastern Europe in late 1989 occurred as the Pentagon was reviewing the drug plans submitted by the commanders-in-chief. Members of the military acknowledged to the press that the imminent threat of reduced budget projections and of force cuts were key in the military's new stance. One two-star general said, "With peace breaking out all over, it might give us something to do."[39]   A high-level Pentagon official said that senior admirals, who first balked at sending ships after drug smugglers, were told that if the Navy stayed out of the drug war, their budget would be cut and they would lose some aircraft carriers. "They like the idea now," said the official.[40]   Admiral William Crowe, former chairman of the Joint Chiefs of Staff, summarized military institutional interests in the drug war this way:

> "Certainly I think we'll put more emphasis on the drug war.
> And if there are resources tied to it, why, you'll see the services
> compete for those, and probably vigorously.
>
> "We take some pride in being accomplished bureaucrats, as
> well as military men.   And I think it's legitimate for military men
> to try and perpetuate their institution..."[41]

One congressional staff member claimed, "It's their new meal ticket now that the commies are not their big threat."[42]   The drug war will never produce the large-scale, multi-billion dollar programs such as the Strategic Defense Initiative or the Stealth bomber, and the Persian Gulf War has removed some steam from the scramble to justify programs through the drug war. However, the military services continue to seek to retain at least some of their endangered budgets and to justify existing technologies through the drug war.[43]

Nevertheless, the majority of general and flag-ranking officers continue to believe that the counter-drug mission is not appropriate for the military.[44]

---

[39] Ibid.

[40] Kevin Merida, "Leaders Sign Declaration against Drugs," Dallas Morning News, February 19, 1990, p. 8.

[41] Admiral William Crowe, Interview on Nightline, January 4, 1990, transcript in Current News: Special Edition, "Military Role in the Drug War," No. 1837, p. 12.

[42] Douglas Waller, "Risky Business," Newsweek, July 16, 1990.

[43] Interview with military analyst familiar with Pentagon anti-narcotics activities, August 1991.

[44] As a result of Secretary Cheney's guidance of September 1989, which was viewed as a signal of the White House's resolve to end the Pentagon's rear-guard resistance, civilian and military leaders within the Department of Defense have publicly displayed a more supportive attitude about the policy.   In public testimony, DOD officials are positive about the efforts being made, and are
(continued...)

In interviews with WOLA, U.S. military officials uniformly state that only a small minority of military officers actively support military involvement in the drug war.[45] Other research shows that, as of late 1990, senior military officials still had "wide-spread doubts and skepticism" about the effectiveness of military involvement in anti-narcotics activities.[46] As Gen. Bernard Loeffke, the chairman of the Inter-American Defense Board told WOLA, "I am one of the very few general officers who supports the drug mission, mainly because of its training benefits [for U.S. troops]."[47] Several military analysts interviewed indicated that the Persian Gulf War, while strengthening military confidence about carrying out any sort of mission, also indicated that the military's "bread-and-butter" for the near future lies in preparation for mid-intensity regional conflicts such as the Gulf war, not the drug war.

However, at the Southern Command, where the probability of mid-intensity conflicts is remote, the drug war serves budgetary interests much more directly. Within the U.S. military, SouthCom is known as the "low-intensity conflict command," and the drug war's priority for the administration represents a significant opportunity to carry out previous activities and to fund research and development in new low-intensity conflict technologies. SouthCom's former Commander-in-Chief, Maxwell Thurman, stressed the opportunities for using existing and new high-tech devices for intelligence-gathering in the drug war. SouthCom officials report that as of mid-1991 SouthCom's Commander-in-Chief, Gen. George Joulwan, had three overall budget priorities -- each a multi-million dollar project related to the drug war: the Command Management System, the Caribbean Basin Radar Network, and an Airborne Low Reconnaissance Program.[48]

The involvement of the U.S. military in the drug war has generated limited institutional momentum in the defense industry around anti-narcotics technology. While most of the demand for new technologies revolves around domestic law enforcement and interdiction purposes, much is also aimed at supporting efforts in foreign countries. Several conferences, held since the

---

[44](...continued)
genuinely satisfied that a role in arrests, searches and seizures at home was averted. See Doug Jehl and Melissa Healy, "In Reversal, Military Seeks Drug War Role," The Los Angeles Times, Dec. 15, 1989.

[45] Interviews were conducted on "background," i.e., with anonymity requested, in early 1991.

[46] Research conducted by Bruce Michael Bagley, of the University of Miami, in over twenty interviews with senior military officials. See ""The Myth of Militarization: An Evaluation of the Role of the Military in the War on Drugs in the Americas," paper presented at Latin America Strategy Development Workshop, organized at the direction of the U.S. Joint Chiefs of Staff by the Institute for National Strategic Studies of the National Defense University, September 26-29, 1990, p. 102.

[47] Interview with Gen. Bernard Loeffke, May 2, 1991. Gen. Loeffke was commander of U.S. Army South when it carried out Operation "Blast Furnace" in 1986.

[48] Interviews with SouthCom officials, August 1991.

Andean strategy was announced, have aimed to take better advantage of the opportunities for contracts in the anti-narcotics field.[49] Both the topics and the content of the sessions of these conferences show that military planners are looking into the future and identifying various technological needs for the drug war and for other low-intensity conflict applications.[50] A plethora of technological capabilities are being developed for the drug war. At a conference in May 1991, for example, the Director of the Naval Special Warfare Division, Captain Thomas Steffens, said that "we and our Western allies" have sold our detection devices to Third World militaries and now need equipment to counter our own devices.[51] He also indicated that the "big emphasis" for the future is coastal and riverine operations, mainly because of anti-narcotics activities in Central and South America. Brig. Gen. Running, U.S. Special Operations Command (USSOCOM), said that the "drug war has given us an opportunity to develop LIC-unique systems." While the drug war will never account for more than a tiny portion of overall Defense contracts, important institutional investment in the 'war on drugs' has taken place.

B. The Drug War: A New Military Mission in Latin America

Military officials also acknowledge that the drug war provides certain institutions within the Pentagon with a new mission at a time when the end of the Cold War has removed the 30-year old justification for U.S. security policy in the hemisphere. The attitudes about the anti-drug mission within the Pentagon are indicative. Military opposition has been concentrated on an expansion of an anti-drug mission in the domestic sphere and in border interdiction. The military has maintained a much more positive attitude toward its role in the source countries. The nature of source-country activities is much closer to traditional security assistance functions, carried out principally as part of counter-insurgency programs in Latin America for thirty years, than they are to the law enforcement activities which the military so vigorously opposes. In June 1988, current Chief of Naval Operations Admiral Frank Kelso and then-Secretary of Defense Frank Carlucci both suggested that Congress increase security assistance to Latin America as a means of fighting

---

[49] Contractors have exhibited great interest in big-ticket items, while administration officials have stressed that they do not need high-technology instruments, but low-tech equipment that is "simple, user-friendly and cheap." Quoted from a mid-1990 conference "Drug Summit I," cited in "Ailing Defense Contractors Urged to Arm the Drug War," The Miami Herald, July 15, 1990.

[50] In 1990 and 1991, for example, the Technical Marketing Society of America (TMSA) sponsored periodic conferences on "Special Operations, Low Intensity Conflict and Drug Interdiction," at which U.S. military and civilian officials laid out the concepts and the technological requirements for anticipated low-intensity conflict and anti-narcotics efforts.

[51] See conference, ibid.

the drug war.[52]   In that same testimony, both officials called into question congressional proposals to "seal the borders" and opposed expanding the military's role in domestic law enforcement activities.

Indeed, where new anti-drug activities have converged with previous roles and with assigned responsibilities, entities within the Defense Department have been more enthusiastic about the drug war. That enthusiasm is concentrated in those sectors of the Department of Defense which hold responsibility for "source-country" regions (in this case, Latin America) and for Low-Intensity Conflict.[53]   The Army-Air Force Center for Low Intensity Conflict (CLIC), the principal thinktank on low-intensity conflict within the armed forces, was among the few DOD entities to openly support military participation in the anti-narcotics mission.[54]   It started assisting the DEA with planning in 1988.   One officer of the CLIC said, "We [the CLIC] have always been at the fore in thinking that the military could do more in counter-narcotics. Like the country song goes, 'We were drugs before drugs were cool'."   In addition, military officers report that the Special Operations Command, a unified command created in 1987 by congressional order to strengthen special operations and low-intensity conflict capabilities, has also been supportive of a role in anti-narcotics.[55]

The most enthusiastic sector within the Department of Defense about the war on drugs has been the U.S. Southern Command. SouthCom exercises the principal role in the implementation of the U.S. military role in Central and South America, and has also played the lead role in conceptualizing and planning the military component of the Andean strategy.[56]   SouthCom

---

[52] See footnote #37, Chapter 2.

[53] Several entities within the Department of Defense are involved in anti-narcotics policy in the Andes. The major ones are (1) the office of the Drug Policy Coordinator (DOD's "Drug Czar"), Stephen Duncan, who also serves simultaneously as the Assistant Secretary of Defense for Reserve Affairs, and his staff, who are responsible for overall policy and operations, (2) the Counter-narcotics Unit within the Joint Chiefs of Staff, responsible for facilitating joint operations, (3) the various unified and specified commands, including SouthCom, the Special Operations Command, and the Atlantic Command, (4) the Inter-American Region division (which in early 1991 had a three-person Counter-narcotics unit within the International Security Assistance of the Office of the Secretary), responsible for overall Defense Department policy in Latin America, and (5) the TRADOC, responsible for incorporating anti-drug training curriculum in officer and general educational courses, including CLIC.

[54] The CLIC was founded in 1986 "to serve as the Army-Air Force focal point for military matters relating to low-intensity conflict." It develops LIC doctrine, publishes papers on LIC, and represents "LIC interests" in inter-agency and intra-departmental discussions. It consisted of 28 persons in 1990.

[55] Various interviews, early 1991.

[56] The ten Commanders-in-Chief (or CINCs, pronounced "sinks") of unified and specified commands gained power over their areas of responsibility under the Goldwater-Nichols Reform Act of 1986, which reduced the power of the four service chiefs (The Persian Gulf War is the first war fought under the new system, and the prominence of Gen. Schwartzkopf -- CINC, Central Command -- illustrates the degree of latitude held by the CINCs).

commanders have long advocated an expanded military role in anti-narcotics -
- but in the Cold War context. Even before President Reagan declared drug
trafficking a national security threat in 1986, former SouthCom Commander-
in-Chief General Paul Gorman was pushing for such a declaration.[57] From the
early 1980s, SouthCom was concerned about drug trafficking primarily
because of its perceived relationship with leftist guerrilla movements. The
command was interested in alleged links among narco-traffickers, the
Nicaraguan and Cuban governments, leftist insurgencies, and arms shipments,
and became increasingly interested in these links as relations with Panamanian
President Manuel Noriega soured, impeding SouthCom's ability to operate
from its headquarters in Panama.[58] One former commander of SouthCom said
that every single guerrilla group in Latin America had at some point used
drug trafficking to gain funding for its cause.[59]   And former SouthCom
commander Gen. Fred Woerner, who has opposed many aspects of the drug
war, spoke in favor of expanding the command's role in anti-narcotics-related
security assistance activities when in command.[60]

In contrast to the drug war at home, the drug war in the Andes does not
contradict previous military missions and roles but rather redefines and
expands them into new countries at a time when they had been in question.
The end of the Cold War threw the raison d'etre of the Southern Command
into question. For thirty years the Southern Command has been primarily
engaged in counter-insurgency operations in the hemisphere.[61] The end of the
Cold War removed the decades-long justification for the U.S. military role in
Latin America: fighting communism. Indeed, the end of the war in
Nicaragua, the reduction of U.S. forces in Honduras, and the peace

---

[57] Testimony of General Paul Gorman, former CINCSOUTH, before Senate Subcommittee on
Terrorism, Narcotics, and International Communications, "Drugs, Law Enforcement, and Foreign
Policy: Panama," February 8-11, 1988, p. 44.

[58] Noriega had allegedly been actively involved in all of the aforementioned links.

[59] Testimony of General Paul Gorman, former CINCSOUTH, before Senate Subcommittee on
Terrorism, Narcotics, and International Communications, "Drugs, Law Enforcement, and Foreign
Policy: Panama," February 8-11, 1988, p. 44. At the same time, SouthCom has not responded to
U.S. law enforcement agencies' requests for assistance as promptly as the latter would like.
Congressional investigations revealed that the DEA and the U.S State Department found SouthCom
dragging its feet in certain support roles for these U.S. agencies. However, prior to the Andean
strategy the command favored training and other operational support activities for Andean forces as
necessary to undermine insurgencies.

[60] Telephone interview, February 1991. See also testimony before House Armed Services
Committee, "Military Role in Drug Interdiction," Part 3, September 21, 1989, p. 35.

[61] Because of the absence of conventional threats to U.S. security in the region, there was a
move to eliminate the command in the late 1970s. However, increased U.S. involvement in Central
American "low-intensity conflicts" -- a term which covers a range of low-level military operations
but has meant primarily counter-insurgency in Latin America -- during the 1980s revived the
command's activities. Among the U.S. military's ten unified and specified commands, SouthCom
has a reputation as the "low-intensity conflict" command.

negotiations in El Salvador have signaled an end to what has been SouthCom's central focus for the past decade.

The appointment of General Maxwell Thurman as Commander-in-Chief of SouthCom in mid-1989 indicated the transition of the U.S. military's posture in Latin America from Cold War to Drug War. Following the Panama invasion, Thurman directed his commanders to make counter-narcotics their "number one priority," and organized the command around the anti-narcotics mission.[62] Before Iraq's invasion of Kuwait, Thurman described the drug war as "the only war we've got." A Counter-narcotics Operations Center was established at SouthCom, which reportedly included the command's best officers, and officers were taken off of routine assignments to work on anti-narcotics plans.[63] Before the Gulf war, Thurman put a host of government agencies on the defensive when he requested their assistance in planning anti-drug activities for the Andes, and he generated dozens of proposals.[64] State Department officials acknowledge that SouthCom "jump started" anti-drug efforts, and one Washington analyst familiar with SouthCom described the drug mission as a shark's mouth devouring everything, while the "dorsal fins" addressed issues such as Panama and El Salvador.

In November 1990, Gen. Thurman retired for health reasons, and was replaced by General George Joulwan. Joulwan is not as ardent about the drug war as his predecessor. Under Thurman, the command developed a new list of security threats to the United States. These included not only "drugs" and "insurgencies" but also "underdevelopment," "debt," "immigration," and even "environmental degradation." Joulwan has given added stress to the latter grouping and to an expanded "nation-building" role for the U.S. Armed Forces in Latin America. As Joulwan's political officer said, "The CINC [Joulwan] doesn't want drugs to be the overwhelming objective or mission." Fighting drug trafficking ranks after the command's top objectives of "strengthening democratic institutions" and "regional security."[65]

Nevertheless, informed military analysts report that in practice anti-narcotics operations remain the central role for the Southern Command as of

---

[62] Testimony of General Maxwell Thurman, Commander-in-Chief, U.S. Southern Command, before Senate Appropriations Committee, "Department of Defense Appropriations," March 8, 1990, p. 250.

[63] Interviews with SouthCom officers and well-placed Washington analysts.

[64] These agencies included the Defense Mapping Agency, the military's Center for Low-Intensity Conflict, the Army Rangers, the State Department, the U.S. embassies in the region, and the Corps of Engineers.

[65] Juan O. Tamayo, "From Battling Guerrillas to Pulling Teeth," The Miami Herald, June 14, 1991, p. 22A.

mid-1991, and under Joulwan, SouthCom is proceeding with plans to expand its anti-narcotics efforts in the Andes and throughout Latin America. As one Washington analyst familiar with SouthCom said in early 1991,

"A lot of us had hoped that when George Joulwan took over he would broaden the command's perspective to include other issues. Unfortunately that hasn't happened."

As stated earlier, all three of SouthCom's top overall budget priorities as of mid-1991 are for use in anti-narcotics efforts.

C. Strengthening Military-to-Military Relationships in the Hemisphere

Finally, some officers also acknowledge that the "counter-narcotics mission" converges particularly well with the United States' longstanding perceived interest in maintaining good military-to-military relationships in the hemisphere. Since World War II, the United States Department of Defense has consistently viewed the maintenance of good relations with the militaries of allied Latin American countries as a top priority. In 1978, then-Assistant Secretary of State for Inter-American Affairs, Terence Todman, articulated the function of security assistance:

"The United States for many years has maintained close working ties with the Latin military... This long association has developed an arms relationship with the Latin American countries that has helped us maintain access to their military establishments, a matter of importance since 15 Latin American and Caribbean nations are today governed by or under the aegis of the armed forces. Security assistance to these governments thus is a political tool that provides us an opportunity to exert some influence on their attitudes and actions."[66]

Although the context has changed, the priority assigned to good relations with allied militaries remains unchanged with the Bush administration. In April 1991, then-Under Secretary of State Robert Kimmitt delineated "three basic components of national security strategy". The first component was "defense":

---

[66] In Hearings before House Committee on International Relations, on Foreign Assistance Legislation for FY 1978, pt. 7, p. 68, cited in Lars Schoultz, Human Rights and U.S. Policy Toward Latin America, Princeton University Press, 1981. p. 250.

"First, we need to maintain strong, deployable military forces and **stable military relationships** with our allies around the world.... Moreover, the fact that we possess substantial military resources augments our diplomatic leverage."[67]

In his 1991 Annual Report, Secretary Cheney referred to the need for "Peacetime Engagement," apparently referring to the maintenance of active engagement of the U.S. military with foreign militaries even in peacetime.[68]

These general U.S. security priorities are reflected in U.S. security policy toward Latin America. In June 1989, Spiro Manolas, a leader of the International Military Education and Training (IMET) program, said that the first goal of U.S. training programs in Latin America "is to create rapport with the United States."[69] In interviews, those military officials with responsibilities for U.S. security policy toward Latin America underscore the current need not simply to maintain, but to expand, relations with militaries throughout the hemisphere. For example, one Pentagon official said that, because of the prohibitions on U.S. military aid to Chile, "There's a whole generation of Chilean military officers who have no relation to the U.S. military." "Expanded military relations" is one of seven means listed in SouthCom strategy documents as a means of attaining theater objectives.[70] And in an interview with WOLA, a SouthCom official emphasized that "enhancing military professionalism" is one of the commander-in-chief's top four priorities, stressing that the goal was receiving increasing attention.[71]

Because of the perceived geopolitical interest in strengthening relationships with allies, the end of the Cold War and the spread of civilian rule is seen as opening up new opportunities. U.S. military officials emphasize that for the first time in decades, every country in SouthCom's area of responsibility (which does not include Cuba) is democratic and

---

[67] Amb. Robert M. Kimmitt, then-Under Secretary for Political Affairs, "Economics and National Security," Dispatch, U.S. State Dept., June 3, 1991, p. 398. Emphasis added.

[68] "Peacetime engagement" is not explicitly defined, but is described in the context of anticipating and countering "destabilizing factors" which "undermine weak or embryonic governments and the peacetime conditions that are necessary for democratic institutions to function and mature." Deputy Assistant Secretary of Defense for Inter-American Affairs Nancy Dorn referred to the term "peacetime engagement" in her March 1991 testimony before Congress on U.S. defense policy in Latin America. Secretary Dick Cheney, Annual Report to the President and the Congress, January 1991, p. 6.

[69] Quoted in Tina Rosenberg, "Beyond Elections," Foreign Policy, Fall 1991, p. 89.

[70] Southern Theater Strategy, op cit. "Theatre" refers to the command's entire area of responsibility in this case.

[71] Personal interview, mid-1991.

friendly to the United States.[72] This outlook is embodied in what is SouthCom's overarching strategic goal for the hemisphere, "Vision 2001," or "CINCSO's Vision".[73] "Vision 2001" is defined in SouthCom's Southern Theater Strategy as "a community of free, stable, and prosperous nations, throughout the Southern theater, acting in concert with one another to advance and defend the principles embodied in the Charter of the OAS and the Rio Pact and in concert with U.S. interests" (see Diagram 2.A).[74]

Diagram 2.A

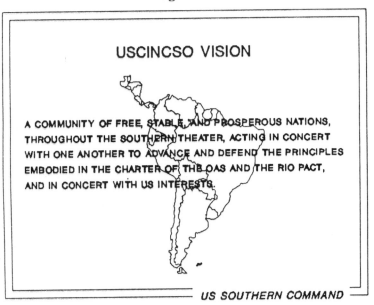

Yet to maintain good military-to-military relationships, the United States must have something to offer, or foreign militaries will have little incentive to be "engaged" with their U.S. counterparts. In the view of U.S. officials, it is too costly not to be engaged. Thus, the provision of security assistance -- money, equipment and training -- is understood not only as the means to further other foreign policy objectives, but as the key to the broader goal of maintaining good military relationships. The U.S. military's term, "enhancing military capabilities," encompasses all of these security assistance tasks.

---

[72] SouthCom officials did not view the government of Suriname as changing the fundamental profile and direction of the hemisphere.

[73] "CINCSO" stands for "Commander-in-Chief South," i.e. the Commander of SouthCom.

[74] "Southern Theater Strategy," unclassified SouthCom document in WOLA files, dated February 12, 1991.

Currently, in SouthCom's view, the U.S. military's part in promoting democracy and achieving "Vision 2001" is neither to work for a reduction in Latin American military forces nor to attempt to delimit the role of armed forces in Latin American societies. Rather, the U.S. military role is to continue to strengthen military capabilities on the assumption that democratic values will be transmitted. "Enhancing host nation capabilities" appears repeatedly throughout SouthCom documents as a goal for counter-insurgency, anti-narcotics, and nation-building activities.[75]

For SouthCom, the Andean strategy represents a new way to offer military assistance that can enhance the ties between the U.S. and Latin American militaries. Public statements by civilian and military officials make it clear that the anti-narcotics mission is part of this goal of augmenting general military capabilities of Andean allies. In 1988, Commander-in-Chief of SouthCom Gen. Fred Woerner said that his most important contribution to the drug war would be "to enhance the host country's military and public security forces in doing their mission within their country."[76] Assistant Secretary of State Melvyn Levitsky said in 1989 that "The military assistance part [of the Andean strategy] is designed to upgrade the capabilities of both militaries and police forces."[77] A member of the U.S. military Group in Colombia explained the need to use anti-drug monies for broader U.S. military activities in that country:

"Up until 1989 there were no restrictions. The aid was coming in under the old MAP [Military Assistance Program]. When the MAP was turned into the FMF [Foreign Military Financing] program, suddenly we had to tie all the aid to counter-narcotics. This presented a problem -- we were pushed into a corner. We have to find ways to justify the aid by trying to tie it to some kind of counter-narcotics purpose. For instance in the military training, not all the courses are related to counter-narcotics, but you can't just shut these programs down."[78]

The convergence of the anti-drug mission with other institutional interests of the U.S. military in the hemisphere raises the possibility that anti-drug aid is

---

[75] See "Southern Theater Strategy," op cit.

[76] Testimony before House Armed Services Committee, Part 3, p. 35.

[77] Testimony before House Foreign Affairs Committee, "Review of the President's Andean Initiative," Nov. 7-8, 1989, p. 17.

[78] Member of U.S. Military group, Bogotá, Summer 1991, in interview conducted by Chris af Jochnick. Jochnick, a 1991 Harvard University Human Rights Fellow from Harvard Law School, conducted the interviews in Colombia between June and August 1991 for a research project on U.S. military assistance to that country. WOLA kindly acknowledges Mr. Jochnick for making the interviews available. Hereafter, "Jochnick interviews".

being used for programs unrelated to counter-narcotics and over which little accountability is exercised. In addition, this convergence could well increase the bureaucratic momentum toward military solutions to a complex social and political issue.

CHAPTER 3

FROM CENTRAL AMERICA TO THE ANDEAN RIDGE: LOW-INTENSITY CONFLICT AND THE WAR ON DRUGS

Chapter Summary

Officials of the Bush administration not only reject assertions that they seek to "militarize" the drug war, but they also object to the notion that they aim to use anti-narcotics programs as a cover for assisting counter-insurgency efforts in the Andes. In their joint report to Congress, required by the Defense Authorization Act of 1990, the Departments of Defense and State said, "The focus of the U.S. effort is counter-narcotics, not counter-insurgency."

Yet the military component of the Andean strategy is historically, doctrinally, and operationally linked to U.S. counter-insurgency strategy. U.S. military documents illustrate that the Pentagon views the counter-drug mission as the latest form of low-intensity conflict and as drawing directly on the strategy and tactics of counter-insurgency. Under what can be called the "narco-guerrilla theory," the administration's military strategy targets new "enemies" -- drug trafficking organizations -- but explicitly includes old enemies -- leftist insurgent groups alleged to have inextricable links to them. The narco-guerrilla theory provides the rationale for the United States to provide Andean forces with equipment, training, and intelligence to augment their counter-insurgency campaigns, which remain their top priority.

It is clear that certain insurgent groups cooperate with drug traffickers. In Peru, coca growers have come to depend upon Sendero Luminoso as intermediaries promoting their interests vis-à-vis the traffickers, and traffickers must deal with the guerrillas.[1] However, most experts see the narco-guerrilla theory as exaggerating the nature of guerrilla-trafficker links and as obscuring important differences in the relationships between traffickers and various insurgent groups. Ultimately the key point of the narco-guerrilla theory -- that counter-narcotics efforts are impossible without counter-insurgency programs -- is not supported by evidence in the case of Colombia. In the case of Peru, the fact that the military component of the Andean strategy consists almost exclusively of counter-insurgency support signifies the need for a separate, careful and public debate on the issue. There remain important contradictions between anti-narcotics activities and counter-insurgency efforts, particularly in

---

[1] It is important to distinguish between coca - a plant with religious, medicinal and cultural uses that has been grown in the Andes for centuries - and cocaine, of which the coca leaf is an ingredient. Likewise, there is a distinction between coca growers - farmers who sell their crop to processors and traffickers -- and drug traffickers.

Peru, where military officials view the U.S.-backed anti-drug mission as undermining efforts against the Sendero Luminoso guerrillas.

The coupling of the military component of the Andean strategy with counter-insurgency efforts has been widely questioned, including by some in the U.S. Congress. Wary of uncritical U.S. support for anti-guerrilla wars, Congress has established restrictions on the use of anti-narcotics monies for counter-insurgency activities. Yet to date, Congress has not fully debated the use of U.S. security assistance for counter-insurgency operations in Colombia and Peru, nor has Congress made the development of adequate monitoring mechanisms a higher priority than the drive to implement drug-related military programs in the Andes.

I. OLD STRATEGIES FOR THE NEW MISSION

Administration officials, including military officers at SouthCom and in the Pentagon, see counter-insurgency as an indispensable component of counter-narcotics. According to recently developed U.S. military doctrine, the U.S. military's relationship to national military and police forces in anti-narcotics activities is identical to its relationship to national forces in counter-insurgency. Between 1988 and 1990, the Center for Low Intensity Conflict (CLIC) drew on a number of presidential National Security Directives and U.S. military manuals to formally define counter-narcotics as a low-intensity conflict mission (see Diagram 3.A).[2] Under low-intensity conflict doctrine, U.S. forces' primary tool is security assistance, which can include training, intelligence support, equipment transfer and maintenance support, and providing advice -- in short the full range of operational support. This doctrine, which reflects the "lessons" of Vietnam about the political difficulties created by U.S. combat deaths, emphasizes the use of national military and paramilitary forces in direct combat roles, with U.S. forces providing support.[3]

More directly, the CLIC also explicates the relationship between anti-narcotics and <u>counter-insurgency</u> (which is defined as one of the four categories within low-intensity conflict, LIC). "Counter-narcotics" is understood to overlap with three of LIC's four operational categories, including "insurgency and counter-insurgency" (see Diagram 3.B). According to a CLIC document called "The Relationship of Counter-narcotics to Low Intensity Conflict," anti-narcotics is one type of counter-insurgency operation.

---

[2] The Center for Low Intensity Conflict's influence should not be exaggerated. It is called on for certain tasks by unified commands and by entities with the Pentagon, including the drafting of doctrine manuals, and is regarded as the main center of thinking on low-intensity conflict. But it is small and not involved in policy or operational decisions.

[3] Low-Intensity Conflict Doctrine, and its relationship to counter-insurgency, are more fully explained in Appendix A, "What Is Low-Intensity Conflict?".

Diagram 3.A

POLICY & DOCTRINAL LINKS

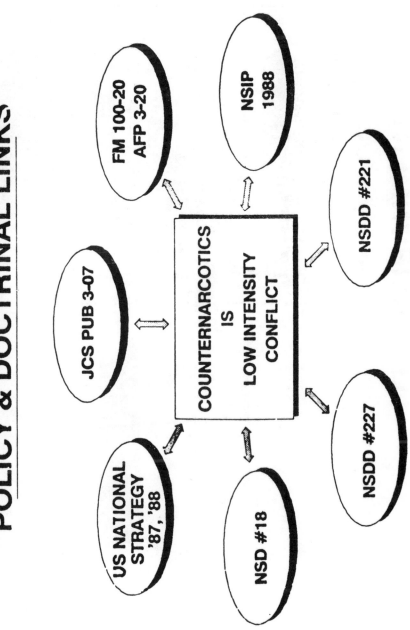

Source: U.S. Army-Air Force Center for Low Intensity Conflict, "Relationship of Counternarcotics to Low Intensity Conflict," Series #11, Army Counternarcotics Symposium. Current as of 1991.

45

Diagram 3.B

LIC ENVIRONMENT

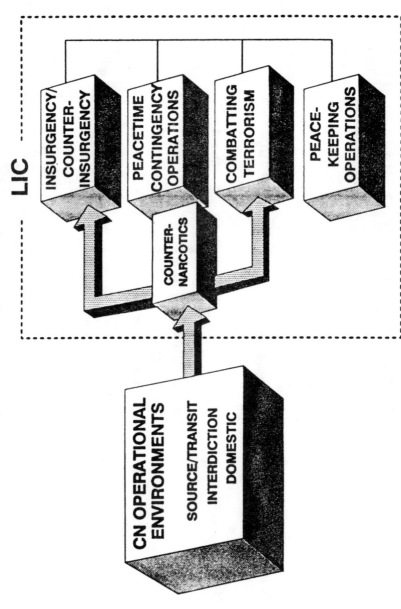

Source: U.S. Army-Air Force Center for Low Intensity Conflict, "Relationship of Counternarcotics to Low Intensity Conflict," Series #11, Army Counternarcotics Symposium. Current as of 1991.

The same diagram shows that every single type of counter-insurgency operation is considered part of the anti-drug mission, including "populace and resources control" (see Diagram 3.C). That is, every kind of activity carried out in Central America as part of counter-insurgency -- training of military forces, intelligence support, logistical support (equipment transfers and maintenance), joint operations, and civic action operations, and "populace control" -- is considered a part of anti-drug efforts in the Andean region.

Military officials confirm that many of their training activities are identical to those carried out in counter-insurgency in Central America.[4] Training activities for Peruvian and Bolivian anti-drug ground police are said to consist of small-unit tactics and other basic soldiering skills given to Light Infantry battalions.[5] Col. Robert Jacobelly, head of all Special Forces trainers in Central and South America, told WOLA that anti-drug training is "basically the same" as counter-insurgency training programs.[6] In drawing up plans for anti-narcotics training programs for Andean military and police forces, the Center for Low Intensity Conflict explicitly drew on "OPATT" follow-up teams (Operational Planning Assistance and Training Teams) in El Salvador, in which small advisory teams remain for twelve to eighteen months with units trained, proposing "OPATTs" for the Andean countries.[7]

---

[4] Indeed, according to a May 1990 article in The Philadelphia Inquirer, many of the same personnel had become involved in the military component of the Andean strategy who were involved in U.S. counter-insurgency and pro-insurgency campaigns of the 1980s in Central America. Col. David Rankin, who served as air attache in El Salvador during the 1984-85 contra resupply operation based there and who reportedly had close ties with operatives of Air Force Maj. Gen. Richard Secord, reportedly was overseeing 30 Air Force officers in INM's air wing in the Andes. In addition, William Olson, former acting Assistant Secretary of Defense for Special Operations/Low Intensity Conflict, was placed in charge of a new INM office for plans and policy.

Other former officials suspected of illegally aiding the Nicaraguan contras were reportedly working in the war on drugs. The Inquirer article reported, "about a dozen veterans of the Reagan administration's illicit effort to aid Nicaragua's contra rebels have volunteered to fight the Bush administration's cocaine war in Peru." These officials include former Special Forces personnel, Richard J. Meadows (said to have advised key figures in the contra supply effort), and Bruce Hazelwood, a retired U.S. Army Delta Force member (formerly posted with Rankin in El Salvador) who coordinated operations in Peru's Upper Huallaga Valley until mid-1990. Institutional or personal factors (e.g., experience in situations of civil conflict, language abilities, etc.) may lie behind the posting to the Andes of people who have served in Central America. However, at the very least, the presence there of such officials illustrates the likelihood that similar counter-insurgency programs and activities will be utilized. See Frank Greve, "Contra Advisers in Peru," May 30, 1990.

[5] See "United States Anti-Narcotics Activities in the Andean Region," Thirty-eighth Report, House Government Operations Report, op cit., p. 15. Also news article....

[6] Interview with WOLA, early 1991.

[7] Interviews with U.S. military personnel, DEA document "Institution Building in the Andes," op cit. One U.S. military officer stated that the OPATT system is unlikely to be used because of lack of resources.

Diagram 3.C

COUNTERNARCOTICS RELATIONSHIP TO INSURGENCIES/ COUNTERINSURGENCIES

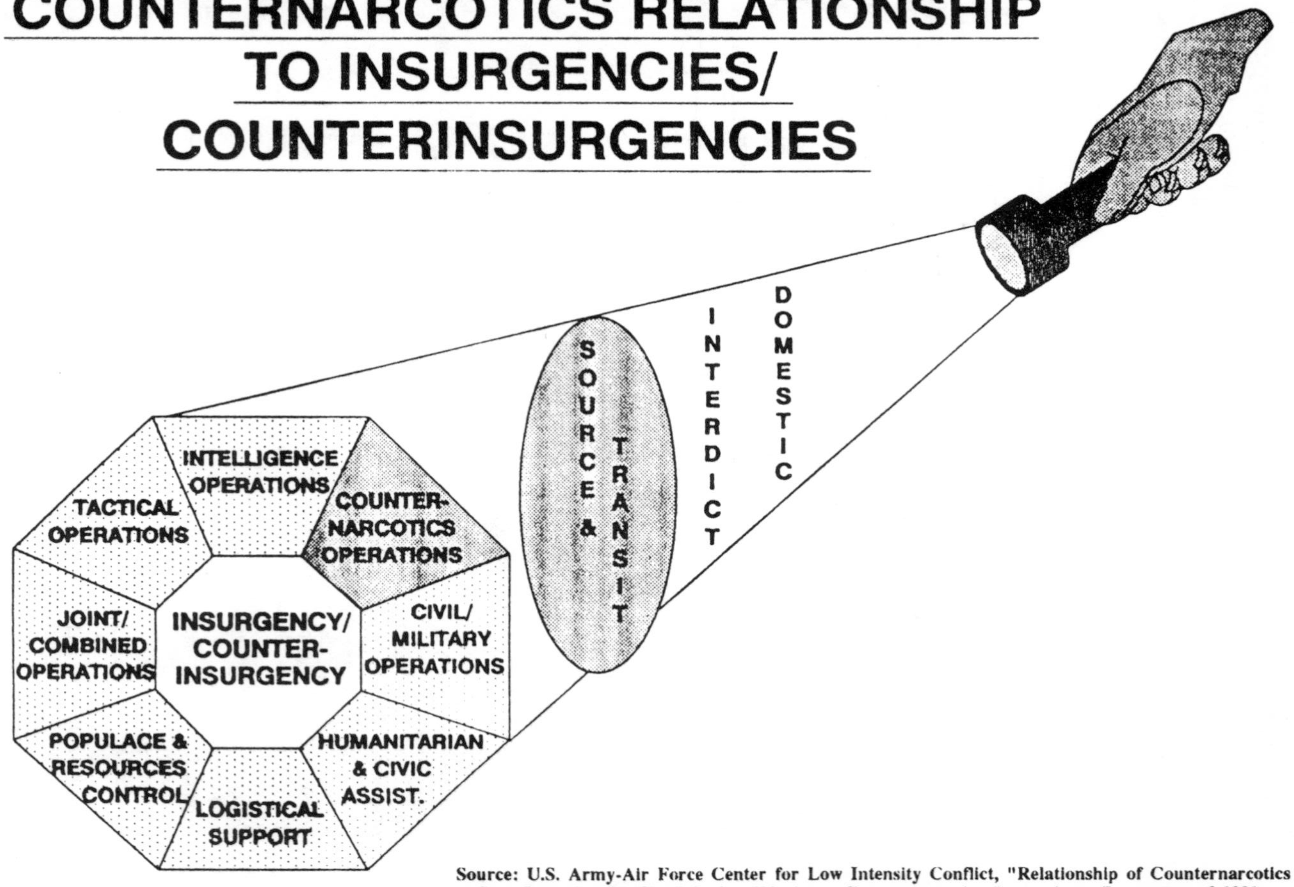

DOMESTIC

INTERDICT

SOURCE & TRANSIT

COUNTER-NARCOTICS OPERATIONS

CIVIL/ MILITARY OPERATIONS

INTELLIGENCE OPERATIONS

HUMANITARIAN & CIVIC ASSIST.

INSURGENCY/ COUNTER-INSURGENCY

TACTICAL OPERATIONS

LOGISTICAL SUPPORT

JOINT/ COMBINED OPERATIONS

POPULACE & RESOURCES CONTROL

Source: U.S. Army-Air Force Center for Low Intensity Conflict, "Relationship of Counternarcotics to Low Intensity Conflict," Series #11, Army Counternarcotics Symposium. Current as of 1991.

SWAIN11

48

II. THE "NARCO-GUERRILLA" THEORY

In U.S. policy, the relationship between anti-narcotics and counter-insurgency is more than just the use of the same training and support activities with national military and police forces. It is based on a set of linked assumptions about the character of international drug trafficking and of the threat it presents to U.S. national security. The "enemies," or targets, of U.S. anti-narcotics activities in the Andes illustrate those links.

On the one hand, administration officials generally think of drug trafficking organizations as the primary targets of drug-related military and paramilitary programs in Latin America, especially in Colombia and Bolivia. The objectives of the Andean strategy convey this emphasis, and hundreds of thousands of dollars have been spent by the Defense Department, the DEA, the National Security Agency, and the CIA to gather intelligence on known and suspected traffickers, their movements, their phone conversations, and their habits. SouthCom and the DEA are most enthusiastic about large-scale raids against numerous trafficker assets, and they have pointed to the raid on Santa Ana, Bolivia, in June 1991 as an example of a successful approach, despite problems with the raid.[8]

On the other hand, the Bush administration -- and the U.S. military -- view the "counter-narcotics mission" as inextricably linked to counter-insurgency in Latin America. The administration has consistently depicted drug traffickers as irrevocably tied to leftist insurgents, justifying the inclusion of "old" enemies in the drug war.[9] In their joint report to the Congress in February 1991, the Departments of State and Defense refer explicitly to "narco-insurgents," explaining, "... we cannot lose sight of the fact that in Colombia and Peru the insurgents are involved in narcotics and, along with traffickers, have created a militarized situation."

Administration officials have been open about their inclusion of counter-insurgency in their anti-narcotics program. In 1990 Assistant Secretary of State for International Narcotics Matters Melvyn Levitsky, said,

---

[8] See WOLA International Drug Policy Brief #4, "A Fundamentally Flawed Policy: The U.S. 'War on Drugs' in Bolivia," September 18, 1991.

[9] The phrase "narco-guerrilla" was first used publicly by U.S. Ambassador to Colombia Lewis Tambs in 1984, when he made the unprecedented claim that the Marxist guerrilla group, the Revolutionary Armed Forces of Colombia (FARC), was working in alliance with the Colombian drug cartels. Although the phrase was widely viewed in Colombia as an attempt to discredit the guerrillas during their peace talks with the government at that time, the Reagan and Bush administrations have continued to stress alleged links between the cartels (especially the Medellín cartel) and leftist insurgent groups. The administration does not use the term "theory".

There is another role for the military in addition to the anti-narcotics role, and that has to do with anti-insurgency. We might as well speak of this frankly.

In the Upper Huallaga valley of Peru for example, you cannot have good counter-narcotics operations unless you have a secure situation in which they can take place. The national police cannot fight the Sendero Luminoso off while they are fighting against the traffickers, and there is this alliance between the Sendero Luminoso and the traffickers so that they mutually support each other, and the Sendero Luminoso profits from that relationship by getting funds to conduct its own struggle against the government. So we recognize that a certain amount of building up the military capabilities has to do with providing a secure environment within the valley, and the same could be said for Colombia, under which strong law enforcement, counter-drug operations can take place."[10]

Other administration statements echo these sentiments. Deputy Assistant Secretary of State for South America Michael Skol said in early 1990, "We are just beginning in Peru. It is the same theory [as in Colombia], the theory that we and the Peruvians cannot fight with law enforcement alone in the Upper Huallaga valley unless the Peruvian military is there fighting the Sendero Luminoso."[11] Increasing host nation counter-insurgency capabilities is part of "counter-narcotics tasks" in the hemisphere, and SouthCom officials strongly object to the notion that insurgents and drug traffickers can be separated.[12]

In the face of congressional concerns that anti-narcotics monies not be spent on unrelated activities, the administration has emphasized that the Andean strategy funding will only be used for counter-insurgency which is in some way related to counter-narcotics. In the case of Peru, the administration has thus far interpreted this restriction geographically, limiting the use of U.S.-provided equipment to regions where coca and cocaine are produced. As Mr. Levitsky said in 1990 (using a double negative),

... we have an interest in helping them fight that insurgency that pertains in that narcotics situation. That does not mean we are

---

[10] Testimony before the Task Force on International Narcotics Control, House Committee on Foreign Affairs, "Review of the President's Andean Initiative," November 7-8, 1989, p. 18.

[11] Testimony before Task Force on International Narcotics Control, House Committee on Foreign Affairs, "Review of the 1990 International Narcotics Control Strategy report," March 1990, p. 142.

[12] See U.S. Southern Command, "Southern Theater Strategy," February 12, 1991. Interviews with Gen. John Ellerson, SouthCom Head of Operations (J-3) and Col. Keith Nightingale, Head of Counter-narcotics, Quarry Heights, Panama, early 1991.

going to try to train...[sic] This does not mean that we are going to assist them in insurgency which not only takes place in the Upper Huallaga valley, but in other places.[13]

As coca and cocaine production shift within Peru and Colombia, the range of counter-insurgency programs considered to be justified under anti-narcotics activities will presumably shift as well.

III. THE NARCO-GUERRILLA THEORY AND COUNTER-INSURGENCY IN THE ANDES

The "narco-guerrilla theory" is likely to be applied in different ways in each of the three Andean Initiative countries. To date there is little evidence by which to judge how U.S. equipment, intelligence, and advice is being utilized by Andean military forces. Hardly any of the main source of U.S. military aid, the Foreign Military Financing program, has been delivered to the Andean armed forces. And in Colombia, where under "drawdown" authority the majority of off-the-shelf U.S. military equipment has been delivered, the classified nature of anti-narcotics operations and the dearth of public monitoring of U.S. assistance make it difficult to reach a conclusive assessment of the relationship between anti-drug aid and counter-insurgency operations. Nevertheless statements by U.S., Colombian, and Peruvian officials provide an idea of how U.S. security assistance is being used in Colombia and is likely to be utilized in Peru.

Colombia

In Colombia, there is evidence that U.S. assistance earmarked for anti-narcotics efforts is going to counter-insurgency programs which appear to be unrelated to anti-narcotics activities. Dr. Alfredo Vázquez Carrizosa, president of the non-governmental Permanent Committee for the Defense of Human Rights and a former Minister of Foreign Affairs, claimed in mid-1991, "U.S. military assistance is not aimed at narco-trafficking; it is only for the guerrilla war."[14] In an interview with congressional staff members of the House Government Operations Committee, Colombian Army Chief-of-Staff Gen. Luis Eduardo Roca and Army General José Nelson Mejía said that $38.5 million of the $40.3 million allocated to Colombia for anti-narcotics assistance in FY 1990 would be used for logistical support for "Operation Tri-Color." Operation Tri-Color, the officers explained, is a three-year counter-insurgency

---

[13] Testimony before House Foreign Affairs Committee, "The Andean Initiative," June 6 and 20, 1990, p. 116.

[14] Jochnick interviews, mid-1991, op cit.

51

operation concentrated in the northeastern part of the country. According to the subcommittee report,

> "When asked by the subcommittee staff to explain how a major military operation in an area not known for its narcotics production could advance the anti-narcotics goals of either country, the military representatives stated that if processing facilities were located during the operation they would be destroyed."

Colombian military officials subsequently denied that the aid would be used in the way described.

However, the interview with the Colombian military officials illustrates the most fundamental reality which shapes U.S. anti-drug programs in that country: The Colombian armed forces' highest priority is not the drug war, but the guerrilla war. For almost thirty years the military has fought leftist insurgent groups. Through peace negotiations with the government, four guerrilla groups have disarmed and reintegrated into civilian political life in the past two years.[15] But the two largest and most powerful insurgent movements, the Revolutionary Armed Forces of Colombia (FARC) and the National Liberation Army (ELN), continue actively to engage government forces and to attack economic infrastructure. Following the December 1990 government attack on the FARC headquarters in La Uribe, and coinciding with the beginning of the Constituent Assembly in February 1991, the FARC and the ELN launched their biggest offensive in years.[16]

In early 1991, then-U.S. Ambassador to Colombia, Thomas McNamara, stated that U.S. anti-drug monies are going to counter-insurgency in Colombia: "on occasion a part of the aid has been used against the guerrillas."[17] More importantly, the Ambassador was quoted in a leading Colombian newspaper as acknowledging that funds from the Andean strategy are going to support "other objectives" than anti-narcotics:

> I don't see the utilization of the arms against the guerrillas as a deviation. The arms are given to the government in order that it may use them in the anti-narcotics struggle, **but also they may be**

---

[15] These groups include the April 19 Movement (M-19), the largest sector of the Popular Liberation Army (EPL), the Revolutionary Workers' Party (PRT), and Quintín Lame (an indigenous-based insurgent group).

[16] "At Least 40 Killed in New Guerrilla Offensive," Madrid EFE, Feb. 5, 1991, and "More on 'Unprecedented Offensive'," Bogotá Inravision Television, Feb. 6, 1991, in Foreign Broadcast Information Service, February 6, 1991, pp. 34-35.

[17] El Espectador, January 28, 1991, cited and translated by Chris af Jochnick, Jochnick interviews, op cit. McNamara remained the ambassador through the Summer of 1991.

used for other objectives. The aid has been used primarily in the offensive against narco-trafficking. Nevertheless, in the [U.S.] Congress from time to time some Senators or Representatives say that **they would prefer that the arms not be utilized in objectives different from the struggle against drugs; but this is not a requirement of the United States.**[18]

The Ambassador's comments appear to directly contradict the International Narcotics Control Act of 1990, and his comments raise questions about the U.S. Embassy's commitment to ensuring that U.S. anti-narcotics assistance be destined only for drug-related activities.

The $65 million "drawdown" in August 1989 is the largest single aid package delivered to date for anti-narcotics in Colombia, and its composition illustrates the institutional interests and mechanisms by which much anti-drug aid is channeled to counter-insurgency programs. President Bush's announcement of the $65 million of equipment from existing Defense Department stocks following the assassination of Senator Luis Carlos Galán was unexpected by the Colombians. According to Colombian and U.S. government officials, U.S. military representatives reviewed a list of needed equipment prepared by the Colombian armed forces and told the Colombians what was available and what the U.S. was willing to provide. Previously the director of the Colombian police Directorate for Anti-Narcotics (DAN) was asked to prepare a list and forward it to the Defense Ministry. According to the director of the DAN, his superiors in the Colombian military made changes to his list and added their own requests.[19]

The resulting list heavily favored conventional military equipment -- useful primarily for counter-insurgency -- not that requested by the police. The armed forces received about 77% of the total emergency aid package, while the police received only 16% (see Table 3.D). This breakdown surprised the Colombian National Police, since it is responsible for between 80-90% of all anti-narcotics seizures and raids on airstrips.[20] Of the equipment, the Colombian Air Force received more than any other service, and much of that total was covered by eight Cessna A-37B "Dragonfly" airplanes. The A-37B is known in armaments literature as a "Counter-insurgency (COIN)" aircraft, and one SouthCom official told WOLA that the

---

[18] El Espectador, August 4, 1991, cited and translated by Chris af Jochnick, Jochnick interviews. Emphasis added.

[19] House Committee on Government Operations, "Stopping the Flood of Cocaine with Operation Snowcap: Is it Working?," House Report No. 101-673, August 14, 1990, pp. 78-80.

[20] Ibid., p. 80.

TABLE 3.D

EMERGENCY ASSISTANCE TO COLOMBIA: $65 MILLION
AUGUST 1989

Breakdown by Recipient of $65 million Emergency Assistance provided to Colombia under Section 506(a). "Drawdown" activity begun August 28, 1989, finished February 1990.

RECIPIENT	AMOUNT	% OF TOTAL
Colombian Air Force	$20,515,743	31.6%
- 3 C-130B Aircraft (from air guard)		
- 8 A-37B Aircraft - 35 M60 Machine Guns		
- 12 Miniguns - 60 M16A2 Rifles		
- 5 M79 Grenade Launchers - 3 Fuel Trucks		
- 3,500 2,75" Rockets - 36 Radios		
- Ammunition and Explosives		
Colombian Army	17,211,993	26.5
- 125 M60 Machine Guns - 290 9MM Pistols		
- 260 M79 Grenade Launchers - 400 M162A2 Rifles		
- 50 M-19 60MM Mortars - 80 Vehicles		
- 25 Inflatables Asault Boats - 160 Radios		
- 50 Night Vision Goggles - Ammunition, Explosives		
Colombian Navy	6,929,115	10.7
- 10,000 M14 Rifles - 80 radios		
- 25 M60 Machine Guns - 30 Vehicles		
- 5 Patrol Boats, 31 ft. - 2 Patrol Boats, 65 ft.		
- 110 M79 Grenade Launchers - Ammunition, Explosives		
Colombian Marines	5,178,131	8.0
Colombian Military Intelligence	7,060	0.0
Colombian National Police	**10,461,025**	**16.1**
- 12 UH-1H Helicopters w/spare parts		
plus Miniguns/M60s		
- 65 M-79 Grenade Launchers - 200 .38 Cal Pistols		
- Ammunition and Explosives - 75 M-60 Machine Guns		
Directorate of Administrative Security	466,827	0.7
- 290 9MM Pistols - 10 M14 RIfles		
- 300 .38 Cal Pistols - 20 Night Vision Goggles		
- Ammunition and Explosives		
Ministry of Justice	170,115	0.3
Shipping and Handling Costs	4,059,991	6.2
TOTAL, SECTION 506(A) ASSISTANCE	**$65,000,000**	**100.0%**

Source: Defense Security Assistance Agency, U.S. Department of Defense.

Dragonfly is "not a counter-narcotics capable aircraft."[21] Colombian research organizations have collected evidence of the use of the A-37B (of which Colombia owns a total of 33, including 25 purchased from the U.S. government since 1978) in counter-insurgency bombardments of civilian populations.[22] In addition, the aid package included 440 grenade launchers, 50 mortars, and 260 M60 machine guns, most of which went to the armed forces (see Table 3.D).

Particularly disturbing, Congress has continued to approve huge amounts of military aid to the Colombian government without any information on the use of equipment provided or its effects in that country. Because U.S. law requires that "drawndown" equipment be delivered within 120 days, most of this equipment has been delivered promptly.[23] However, congressional sources report that virtually none of the Foreign Military Financing funds allocated for FY 1990 and FY 1991 has been delivered to Colombia.[24] The FY 1990-FY 1991 total for military assistance already approved by Congress for Colombia is $125 million. Although the use and effectiveness of this aid is not yet known, the House and the Senate has approved military aid to the Andes for FY 1992. The bulk of all approved military aid is destined for the armed forces rather than the anti-narcotics units of the police. The Colombian military appears to be proceeding with plans to use that aid for counter-insurgency efforts, without any apparent dissent from the administration. Indeed, when queried by congressional staff members in March 1990 about the use of U.S. narcotics-related assistance for counter-insurgency, the U.S. military attaché in Bogotá replied that it is generally understood that the aid is to be used to control both drug trafficking and insurgent activity and that it is not U.S. policy to tell the Colombians how to use U.S. assistance.[25]

Peru

The United States has already been providing training to the Peruvian military for what appear to be counter-insurgency programs, although on a small scale. Since 1987, eighty-one Peruvian military personnel have been trained at the U.S. Army School of the Americas in Ft. Benning, Georgia. Almost half of these received training in psychological warfare, a key

---

[21] WOLA interview in early 1991.

[22] Accounts by witnesses were collected by CINEP, a Colombian research center, and by the Congregación Intercongregacional de Justicia y Paz.

[23] See Sec. 551, Public law 01-167, 1990.

[24] Statements by staff member for the House Foreign Affairs Committee at "Symposium on Special Operations, Low-Intensity Conflict, and Drug Interdiction," May 1991, Washington, DC, and conversations with congressional staff members, mid-1991. While contracts have been issued for equipment with FY 1990 and some FY 1991 appropriations, the content is not yet known.

[25] "Stopping the Flood...," op cit., p. 81.

component of counter-insurgency programs.[26] In addition, the head of all Special Forces in Latin America told WOLA that his men were carrying out a classified operation inside that country, not related to anti-narcotics programs, with Peruvian armed forces.[27] As of this writing, the United States has provided the Peruvian armed forces with no drug-related training under the Andean Initiative.

The link between U.S. anti-narcotics policy and counter-insurgency in Peru is clearer than in Colombia, though still incipient. As illustrated in administration statements cited above, U.S. officials view the military component of the Andean strategy in Peru as consisting principally of helping increase the Peruvian military's capability to fight Sendero Luminoso. U.S. officials invoke the narco-guerrilla theory here more than in any other country, largely because the Sendero Luminoso guerrillas have a strong presence in the largest coca-growing area in the world -- the Huallaga valley. Although the administration would like to see the armed forces involved in anti-drug raids in conjunction with Peruvian police agents, all indications from both governments are that the Peruvian armed forces' role in the drug war is to create a "security umbrella" for anti-drug operations by fighting the guerrillas.

The administration announced its plans for the U.S. military aid package for Peru in early 1990. Those plans were drawn up by the Army-Air Force Center for Low Intensity Conflict in conjunction with SouthCom. According to U.S. Embassy officials in Lima, the proposed package included basic military equipment -- weapons, ammunition, food supplies, uniforms, and other gear -- as well as riverine patrol boats, training for six strike battalions (the primary military forces in coca-producing regions), and the construction of at least one additional base.[28] In addition, 27 A-37 Dragonfly airplanes of the Peruvian Air Force would be refurbished and rearmed. One SouthCom official questioned the reasoning behind creating the strike battalions, describing them as "inappropriate" for anti-narcotics efforts.[29]

While the recent Peru-U.S. accord on military assistance signed in mid-1991 departs from the plans somewhat, the agreement endorses the counter-insurgency thrust of U.S. military assistance in that country. According to a U.S. official, the Fujimori administration successfully requested that about a third of the $34.9 million military aid package for FY 1991 go to civic action

---

[26] From Close-Out Reports, U.S. Army School of the Americas, 1987-1990.

[27] Interview with Col. Robert Jacobelly, Head of SOCSOUTH, Panama, February 1991.

[28] See Frank Greve, "Contra Advisers in Peru," The Philadelphia Inquirer, May 30, 1990. Also interviews of Embassy personnel by WOLA staff member, 1990.

[29] Personal interview, early 1991.

56

programs in the Huallaga valley. In addition, the number of strike battalions to be trained in the first year of assistance was reduced to two from the six originally planned.[30] However, the agreement states that, "counter-insurgency actions are a justifiable component of counter-narcotics activities." The refurbishing of the A-37s and the provision of spare parts for the airplanes are included in the package. The recent accord marks the first overt U.S. support for Peru's counter-insurgency campaign, and training and drug-related aid will begin during 1991.

Bolivia

Even in Bolivia, anti-narcotics programs are viewed as linked to counter-insurgency by some U.S. military officers. Most officials acknowledge that the absence of an active insurgent movement in Bolivia since civilian rule was re-established in 1982 makes the narco-guerrilla theory less applicable to Bolivia. The former U.S. Ambassador to Bolivia, Robert Gelbard, has rejected the characterization of U.S. anti-narcotics activities as "low-intensity conflict" because "there is no war taking place."

However, some military officials view the strengthening of the armed forces and the repression of coca processing and growing to be necessary to preclude insurgent activity. Col. Robert Jacobelly told WOLA that,

> "there is more of a latent insurgency in Bolivia at this point. Things will get worse, and that's related to the drug trade. I think that unless we provide counter-insurgency assistance [to Bolivia] the insurgency will get worse...."[31]

As in Peru, training activities with the police and with the two army battalions have the same basic training content as counter-insurgency training courses.

In addition, civic action programs are more extensive in the case of Bolivia. These programs have long been considered a part of counter-insurgency strategy (see Diagram 3.C). They involve building a better image for government forces among civilian populations by providing services such as health and roads. In addition, civic action programs permit the establishment of intelligence networks on the local level. While the narco-guerrilla theory is not utilized very often with respect to Bolivia, the perceived link among some officers between anti-drug programs and potential unrest is cause for concern about the ultimate result of an expanded U.S. military role.

---

[30] Information provided on background, mid-1991.

[31] Interview with WOLA, early 1991.

IV. UNRAVELLING THE NARCO-GUERRILLA THEORY

The narco-guerrilla theory has been challenged by most experts for overstating the nature of insurgent and trafficker links and omitting the conflictive aspects of traffickers' relationships to all of the guerrilla groups in the region. Most importantly, the theory ignores differences between trafficker relationships with various insurgent groups, as well as links between certain traffickers and other important actors such as Andean military and paramilitary sectors.

In fact, the relationships between traffickers and insurgent groups vary from country to country, shift over time, and are generally better understood as "links" comparable to other ties maintained by traffickers with other actors rather than "alliances." Ultimately the theory's assumption that counter-insurgency is necessary for anti-narcotics is unsustainable in Colombia. In the case of Peru there are important contradictions between the drug war and counter-insurgency efforts.

Colombia

Certain Colombian guerrilla groups have at times cooperated with drug traffickers. There is evidence that the FARC levies war taxes on the trafficking of cocaine and on the wages of coca growers in the southern and eastern Llanos region of the country.[32] The FARC is also accused by U.S. and Colombian authorities of owning its own cocaine production facilities and of protecting the laboratories and plantations of the traffickers.[33] Some officials point to the fact that many files relating to narcotics trafficking were burned as evidence that drug traffickers backed the M-19's takeover of the Palace of Justice in 1985. It is true that these files were burned -- but so were a great many others having nothing to do with drug-related cases.

In Colombia, there is no evidence that military or law enforcement operations against drug traffickers require operations directed against leftist insurgents. One European diplomat in Bogotá, for example, said:

> I don't think military support is crucial at all to the counter-
> narcotics police efforts. I've been to places where the army

---

[32] Rensselaer W. Lee III, The White Labyrinth, Transaction Publishers, New Brunswick, NJ, 1989, p. 166.

[33] The U.S. State Department reports that 31,000 hectares of coca leaf were produced in Colombia in 1990, a relatively small number relative to the 138,000-plus hectares of higher quality coca under cultivation in Peru and 56,500 in Bolivia (Estimates based on other methodologies yield much higher numbers of hectares under cultivation for Peru and Bolivia). Most coca leaf production takes place in the southeastern plains region of the country.

frustrates police, where they're actually guarding the labs. You don't need the army to take out labs. The police are capable and have been doing it on their own. I've noticed no increased commitment on the part of the army to go after traffickers."[34]

In addition, the narco-guerrilla theory exaggerates the strength and relative importance of cooperation between certain guerrillas and traffickers. Colombian drug traffickers' links with right-wing paramilitary squads have been more extensive and significant than cooperation with insurgents. At times these links have constituted alliances involving common strategizing and joint operations. In the early 1980s, drug cartels began investing in large land parcels in the countryside. As of 1990, they were estimated to control about one million of the 13 million hectares under cultivation in Colombia.[35] With the new acquisition of land, many traffickers came to share the interest of local land and ranch owners in eliminating leftist opposition and rising guerrilla kidnappings and extortion.[36]

To do this, they joined forces with large landowners in the region, who organized paramilitary squads -- often with advice, financing, and arms provided by the armed forces. Hired killers, called *sicarios*, who had been trained in schools organized and funded by cartel leaders such as Pablo Escobar and Gonzalo Rodríguez Gacha, increasingly participated in these squads. In the Middle Magdalena region, this alliance between drug traffickers and paramilitary death squads was effective in reducing the guerrilla presence -- and in killing or driving out almost all advocates of socio-economic change. One Colombian historian refers to this alliance as "narcoparamilitarism".[37]

Indeed, hostility and violence have been the dominant characteristics of the relationship between insurgents and traffickers for several years. Following the M-19's kidnapping in 1981 of Martha Nieves Ochoa, sister of a leading Medellín cartel leader, the cartel and landowners created a death squad known as Muerte a Secuestradores (MAS -- "Death to Kidnappers") to

---

[34] Jochnick interview with diplomat who requested anonymity. Mid-1991.

[35] According to Columbia University Professor Marc Chernick, "To put that in historical perspective, Colombia has had a land reform program for about 25 years, in which the state has distributed 900,000 hectares. During the past ten years, the predominant tendency has been a 'counter-land reform,' with more land passing into the hands of the drug traffickers than has been distributed to the peasants." Figures and quote from Marc Chernick, Colombia's "War on Drugs" vs. the United States' "War on Drugs", WOLA International Drug Policy Brief #3, May 1991. See also "El narco-agro," Semana, 29/nov/88-5/dic/88.

[36] For more information, see WOLA, Colombia Besieged: Political Violence and State Responsibility, (Washington, D.C.: November, 1989).

[37] See Carlos Medina Gallego, Autodefensas, Paramilitares y Narcotráfico en Colombia, Editorial Documentos Periodísticos, 1990.

strike back at the M-19 and its perceived supporters. Throughout the 1980s, the principal victims of the MAS were civilian leaders of local unions and peasant associations and others suspected of supporting the guerrillas. Traffickers and their private armies have primarily targeted suspected guerrilla sympathizers. Drug trafficking has stimulated an enormous amount of non-political violence (e.g., killings in intra-cartel turf wars, bombings, and kidnapping of wealthy civilians) However, the majority of drug-related political violence has affected leftist civilians and guerrilla organizations rather than government officials and members of the traditional parties.

Government forces have been important allies of right-wing paramilitary squads and of drug traffickers. Between 1965 and 1989, Colombian Legislative Decree 3398 authorized the armed forces to organize "self-defense groups" on the local level which would serve to augment government anti-guerrilla efforts. However, paramilitary squads, which engage in offensive operations and frequently include active and former military officers, have used the law to masquerade as self-defense groups. In 1983 the Attorney General of Colombia indicted 59 active-duty military officers and soldiers for membership in the MAS.[38] Examples of massacres of peasant activists by paramilitary squads with direct links to cartel leaders include the killing of 20 peasants in the Urabá region in March 1988, the murder of 36 peasants in La Mejor Esquina in April 1988, and the massacre of 42 peasants in Pueblo Bello in January 1990.[39]

In the last two years, the Colombian government has recognized this danger from the right and attempted to dismantle paramilitary groups. In April 1989, in the face of rising violence by such forces, President Barco issued decrees aimed at curbing paramilitary activity.[40] This resulted in highly-publicized raids of paramilitary training schools. In early 1991

---

[38] See Medina Gallegos, op cit., pp. 186-87.

[39] See Lee op cit., p. 160-161, and Americas Watch, The "Drug War" in Colombia: The Neglected Tragedy of Political Violence, 1990.
    One of the most striking examples of collaboration between drug traffickers, paramilitary squads and the military is the case of Pueblo Bello. In that case, 42 peasants were taken by a 52-member paramilitary squad to a ranch where they were tortured and killed in January 1990. An inquiry confirmed that the two trucks carrying the peasants and most of their armed captors passed two army roadblocks on their way to the ranch. Disciplinary proceedings were instigated against the commanders of the roadblocks. The killings were said to have been ordered by landowner Fidel Castaño, on whose ranch the bodies were found. Castaño is accused by U.S. officials of having replaced Gonzalo Rodríguez Gacha as the military leader for the Medellín cartel after the former was killed by Colombian authorities in December 1989. See Americas Watch, op cit. Castaño has recently disbanded his paramilitary squad after the demobilization of the EPL in the area, a reported personal conversion, and publicity over the Pueblo Bello investigation.

[40] Among other things, the decrees created a specialized police unit aimed at paramilitary groups and ended the army's authority to distribute arms to civilians.

60

Colombian officials reported that the government had eliminated paramilitary squads in the country.[41]

Unfortunately, this is not true. Paramilitary groups continue to operate and maintain their links to military personnel. In a mid-1991 interview, Colombia's Procurador General (equivalent of Attorney-General), Dr. Carlos Arrieta, said,

> "The paramilitary groups are the most serious problem that we have with the military. In many cases the army acts through these groups which makes it hard to convict them [the military]."[42]

The paramilitary collaboration with drug traffickers continues, although it has evolved. The army's collaboration with, and implicit support of, paramilitary groups has continued. In April 1991, one of the country's best-known paramilitary leaders, Henry de Jesús Pérez, gave an unprecedented interview in which he detailed not only the longstanding links between the army and paramilitary squads of which he had been a leader, but also ongoing close cooperation -- including joint operations -- between his paramilitary group and police forces. According to Pérez, the target of this collaboration as of 1991 was Pablo Escobar, with whom Pérez had cooperated for years. Pérez claimed that he disagreed with Escobar over the cartel's violent campaign against the state. It is inconceivable that the paramilitary squads could continue to operate without at least the consent, if not the sponsorship, of certain regional military commanders.[43]

In addition to traffickers' links to paramilitary groups in operations against leftist leaders and organizations, the cartels' relationship with corrupt government officials parallel their relationships with the FARC, as well as to Sendero Luminoso and the MRTA in Peru. Just as traffickers pay insurgent groups to be able to operate unimpeded in certain zones, they make payments to certain officials of each Andean government for free access to airstrips, roads, rivers and information. Those funds are generally destined for individual officers as bribes rather than organizational ends. Nevertheless, the ties that traffickers have with government officials are in no way less "inextricable" than alleged cooperation with certain guerrilla organizations.

---

[41] Gabriel Silva, Special Adviser to President Gaviria, in meeting with WOLA, February 14, 1991. See also article by Douglas Farah, The Washington Post, early 1991.

[42] Jochnick interviews, mid-1991, op cit.

[43] See Americas Watch, The "Drug War" in Colombia: The Neglected Tragedy of Political Violence, 1990. Pérez was assassinated in July 1991, presumably by men hired by Pablo Escobar.

Peru

Although Peru appears to be the place where the narco-guerrilla theory is most applicable, Peru also demonstrates most vividly the problems of applying the narco-guerrilla theory in practice. Because coca-growing is so important to the economy in conflictive areas of Peru, there are fundamental contradictions between what is required for successful counter-narcotics operations, on one hand, and counter-insurgency, on the other. Unlike Colombia, Peru is principally a site of coca leaf production rather than cocaine processing and trafficking. The Maoist Sendero Luminoso guerrillas exercise extensive influence in the Upper Huallaga valley, the world's most productive coca cultivation area. They serve as intermediaries between cocaine traffickers, many of whom come across the border from Colombia, and Peruvian coca producers. The MRTA (Túpac Amaru Revolutionary Movement) is reported to play a similar role in its areas of influence.[44] The guerrillas gain revenue by taxing coca and coca-based products in transit, and they gain support among the peasants by ensuring certain price standards and by protecting the producers from eradication efforts. In addition, there are reports that the Sendero Luminoso coerce peasants in some areas to grow coca plants.[45]

Sendero Luminoso's relationship with drug trafficking organizations (of which few are based in Peru) is thus one of tension, as the former cut into the latter's profits. Analysts agree that, in this way, the Sendero Luminoso has rapidly gained support among coca growers in the coca-producing areas of the Huallaga valley, and that they are now building support in emerging coca-producing zones in the Ene, Ucayali, Tambo and Apurímac river valleys.[46]

Peruvian military officials object to the logic of the narco-guerrilla theory, pointing to the contradictions between fighting drug traffickers and fighting Sendero Luminoso in coca-growing regions. Military officials believe that it will be impossible to gain the support of the local population required to undercut the Sendero Luminoso if military personnel are also attacking the economic base of the region through anti-narcotics. operations. They understand this trade-off from first-hand experience. The military commander of the zone covering the Upper Huallaga valley between April and December 1989, Gen. Alberto Arciniega, embraced a "hearts and minds" counter-insurgency strategy which emphasized winning local support for the military's battle against Sendero Luminoso. Gen. Arciniega explicitly rejected the anti-narcotics mission for the army and endorsed the local coca growers federation.

---

[44] See U.S. State Department, INCSR, March 1991, p. 120.

[45] Ibid.

[46] Ibid.

62

His stance angered U.S. officials, who accused him of being involved in drug trafficking.[47]

One of Gen. Arciniega's successors, Gen. Mario Brito Romero, expressed his conviction that counter-insurgency is incompatible with the drug war:

"If we attack drug trafficking, we will convert the local population into our enemy... Then instead of one enemy, Sendero, we will have three: Sendero, the local population who will then support Sendero, and the drug traffickers, who will then provide resources to Sendero."[48]

In an interview, Gen. Brito maintained that U.S. military aid would be acceptable only for counter-insurgency purposes and only if a significant economic aid package were included.[49]

In fact the Peruvian armed forces cooperate with traffickers in ways which may be more significant than the protection Sendero Luminoso provides coca growers. Although the narco-guerrilla theory relies on the fact that guerrillas exact payments for permitting coca to be produced and transported, U.S. officials confirm that in the Upper Huallaga valley, the Peruvian military also takes payments for protecting airstrips and roads. In Uchiza, the military is reportedly paid for each airplane allowed to land on a commercial airstrip under the supervision of military personnel. Peruvian military units have actually fired on local police and U.S. DEA agents in the UHV. A report by the House Government Operations Committee notes that:

"In two separate incidents during the second week of March 1990, Peruvian police units travelling over the UHV in INM-owned helicopters were fired upon by military personnel. In both instances, the police helicopter was traveling from Tingo María to Santa Lucía on routine maintenance runs when it observed a trafficker's Cessna approaching an airstrip in the town of Ramal de Aspuzana where Peruvian military officers were waiting. The helicopter flew close enough to scare the plane into flying off in a northerly direction toward the town of Tocache. The helicopter was low on fuel and was unable to follow the plane. On the helicopter's return trip to Tingo María, the crew heard automatic

---

[47] The U.S. Embassy has never substantiated the charges. However, there is ample evidence that military personnel have, and continue, to accept payments from drug traffickers to use military-controlled public and private airstrips under direct military supervision.

[48] General Brito's comments were made in October, 1990 in a meeting with a World Council of Churches' delegation which included a WOLA staff member.

[49] Personal interview with WOLA staff member, October 1990.

weapon fire and the door gunner saw military personnel in the hills firing at their helicopter."[50]

Local residents often claim that military personnel close off the main highway through the area to allow Colombian traffickers' planes to land. Once the coca paste is loaded and the money exchanged, the road blockade is removed.

V. CONGRESS AND COUNTER-INSURGENCY

Members of Congress continue to express concern that anti-narcotics assistance be used for the purposes intended. In early 1990, one Congress member objected to claims by Assistant Secretary of State Michael Skol that the U.S. interest in fighting drug trafficking and the Peruvian interest in fighting insurgents "converged" in the Upper Huallaga valley.[51] Representative Larry Smith (D-FL), then-chair of the House Task Force on International Narcotics Control, said:

> Mr. Skol, what is this convergence of interests? I never heard of that before. We have specific rules regarding the use of American aid only to designated anti-narcotics units of the military....
>
> I mean, if you are talking about this assistance somehow bleeding over out into the military then you are signing the death warrant for this program. Because Congress is not going to go back on the conditions it imposed before.[52]

Mr. Smith was referring to conditions imposed in the authorizing legislation which specifies that anti-narcotics monies be used only for narcotics-related activities. The International Narcotics Control Act of 1990 strengthened oversight of those conditions, requiring the President specify in writing to Congress: 1. the country; 2. the type and value of the assistance; 3. the law enforcement or other units that will receive the FMF funds; and, 4. an explanation of how the proposed assistance will further counter-narcotics purposes.[53]

The Bush administration has stated that it has taken steps to ensure accountability through "end-use monitoring" of U.S. equipment sent through

---

[50] From "Stopping the Flood of Cocaine...", op cit., p. 38.

[51] Michael Skol, op cit, March 1990, p. 143.

[52] Hearings before the House Task Force on International Narcotics Control, of the House Foreign Affairs Committee, "Review of the 1990 International Narcotics Control Strategy Report" March 1990, pp. 143-144.

[53] Section 4(b), International Narcotics Control Act of 1990.

the anti-narcotics program, while simultaneously admitting the difficulty of such monitoring. End-use monitoring is provided for in the bilateral agreements with each of the Andean countries and "is performed when necessary" according to the Departments of Defense and State.[54] "The administration is taking steps to ensure that equipment and training provided for counter-narcotics is being used for the purposes intended."[55] One U.S. embassy official in Lima said that the DEA usually accompanies anti-narcotics raids and can thereby monitor equipment use.[56]

At the same time, U.S. officials admit that accountability is extremely difficult. One U.S. embassy official in Bogotá said, "The distinction between counter-insurgency and counter-narcotics is hard to make. It's not so terrible if the military is pursuing counter-insurgency to protect the Colombian democracy. We are definitely getting our money's worth out of the military."[57] Privately, Defense Department officials and SouthCom officers confirm that it is practically impossible to ensure that anti-narcotics equipment is going only to drug-related operations. They point out that the Colombian armed forces already had the same models of the UH-1H and the A-37B's provided under the Andean strategy. One official said, "How can you expect a soldier to stop before he shoots a guerrilla and say, 'Wait a minute. Is this my counter-narcotics clip or my counter-insurgency clip?' Especially when the guerrilla may be trafficking drugs, etc."

Despite the administration's statements, Congress continues to have concerns about the ability to monitor anti-drug monies. While it has generally accepted administration claims that some counter-insurgency is a necessary part of counter-narcotics, it has found mechanisms for end-use monitoring insufficient. A report by the House Government Operations Committee in late 1990 found "a lack of effective controls to ensure that anti-narcotics assistance is not used to fund counter-insurgency campaigns."[58] The report found that in Colombia "there is evidence that anti-narcotics military aid has been inappropriately used for counter-insurgency purposes," and the chair of that committee said, "One of the committee's most significant and alarming findings is that our government may be giving drug aid as a smokescreen to block insurgencies."[59] In mid-1991, the U.S. Senate was considering a provision passed by the House of Representatives which would

---

[54] Joint report to Congress, transmitted February 1991, op cit.

[55] Ibid.

[56] Meeting with WOLA staff, mid-1991.

[57] Jochnick interviews, op cit., Summer 1991.

[58] House Committee on Government Operations Report 101-991, November 30, 1990, p. 47.

[59] Representative John Conyers, quoted in news release by House Committee on Government Operations, December 21, 1990.

forbid assistance to Peru's National Police Counter-insurgency Unit (the "Sinchis") because that unit is "not a law enforcement unit that is organized for the specific purpose of narcotics enforcement," but is instead a "commando-type anti-terrorist unit" with a "well-documented history of brutal human rights abuses."[60] The House Government Operations committee report concluded, "Effective controls must be developed to ensure that counter-narcotics assistance is not being used for counter-insurgency purposes."

---

[60] See Section 762(f) of HR 2508, the "International Cooperation Act of 1991," and accompanying report language for the House Foreign Affairs Committee, June 4, 1991, p. 183.

CHAPTER 4

IMPLEMENTING THE ANDEAN STRATEGY

Chapter Summary

Although the five-year Andean Initiative is now in its third year, much of the Andean strategy's military component is only in its initial stages. Congressional sources report that, except for "drawndown" equipment, virtually none of the military assistance allocated for FY 1990 and FY 1991 has been delivered. Training of Bolivian army troops began only in mid-1991, and drug-related U.S. security assistance programs in Peru were inaugurated only in May 1991, when the bilateral anti-drug accord was signed. SouthCom's intelligence network is not yet fully installed, and the Pentagon is in the early stages of what it views as a multi-year comprehensive program in counter-narcotics.

A number of factors have delayed the execution of the Andean strategy. The Persian Gulf War focused the attention of all the U.S. agencies involved in foreign policy on the Middle East and temporarily drew some equipment away from interdiction and other anti-narcotics programs in Latin America. The Andean strategy has also run into the opposition of governments in the region. In Bolivia and Peru both the civilian governments and the army leadership have until recently openly resisted army participation in the war on drugs. Against the military thrust of U.S. strategy, the Bolivian and Peruvian governments have consistently claimed that, rather than forcing peasant coca growers to abandon the crop through interdiction and eradication programs, they should be offered positive incentives to switch to viable alternative crops. And, like the U.S. military, the armies of both countries have viewed drug control as a police function, of lower priority than external defense and anti-subversion. Colombia has strongly opposed any high-profile role for U.S. advisers.

Nevertheless, implementation of much of the military component of the Andean strategy is now underway. U.S. drug-related military training of police forces, begun before the announcement of the Andean strategy, continues. The Command Management System is being expanded, and most of the Caribbean Basin Radar Network (CBRN) radars are operational. U.S. military teams are planning and coordinating drug raids in Bolivia and Peru. In Colombia, Peru and Bolivia, all three national services -- the Army, Navy and Air Force -- have now signed on to the drug war. Even with the surrender of top drug leader Pablo Escobar, his lieutenants in Colombia, and the top three traffickers in Bolivia, U.S. military training and support activities continue to go forward. Large-scale raids have been conducted in Bolivia, and recently-trained army personnel have already participated in drug-related operations. The Peru-U.S. anti-narcotics accord has opened the door for long-standing plans to go forward in that country. In mid-1991, overflights by AWACS radar planes began over Peru, and the U.S. announced that Special Forces would be sent to that country as trainers in fighting traffickers and the Sendero Luminoso. Indeed, with the end of the Persian Gulf War the Pentagon has refocused attention on the drug war, and is now broadening its anti-narcotics programs to include Central America and the rest of South America.

I. THE MILITARY ROLE AND U.S.-ANDEAN DIPLOMACY

The Andean strategy explicitly recognizes that the political will of Andean governments is fundamental even to get anti-narcotics projects off the ground. However, these governments do not have the same concerns and priorities as the U.S., and these differences have surfaced during the first two years of the Andean strategy. The administration has recognized the problems caused by the differences: "[W]e have been disappointed with the efforts of some countries and with our own inability to cooperate with them."[1] The Colombian government's outcry over the proposed carrier group and the spurning of any U.S. combat troops illustrate some of the limits that Andean governments have placed on U.S. anti-narcotics policy.

Andean governments have been cool, or directly opposed, to some of the most fundamental elements of the U.S. strategy. Bolivia and Peru have insisted that the economic component of the Andean strategy be given greater weight and resisted involving their national armies in anti-narcotics activities. Only after intense U.S. pressure and months of delay, did the two countries sign bilateral accords which acceded to army involvement in the drug war. In both cases, the United States made concessions but succeeded in retaining what it regards as the key elements of the military component of the strategy: training of armed forces, provision of equipment and advice on anti-narcotics raids, coordination of intelligence activities, and military integration into broader anti-cocaine programs. Colombia has readily accepted the influx of U.S. security assistance, including large amounts of equipment and a training and advisory role for the U.S. military. However, the Colombian government has also expressed a willingness to forego economic as well as military assistance in exchange for trade benefits with the United States.

---

[1] Assistant Secretary of State Melvyn Levitsky, in hearings before the House Foreign Affairs Committee, "Review of the 1991 International Narcotics Control Strategy Report," March 5, 7, 12, 13, 1991, p. 3.

BOLIVIA

Despite the early involvement of the U.S. troops in anti-narcotics activities in Bolivia, the government there has struggled to give a greater economic emphasis to the Andean strategy and tried to draw the line at involving its own army in the war on drugs. A Bolivian official testified in 1990,

> ...now is also the time for the government of the United States to consider granting additional cooperation to Bolivia for fiscal year 1990, which should **ideally come in the form of economic, rather than military, assistance. But if it is to be military assistance, then it would help our efforts more if the emphasis is not on a new role for the army in interdiction and/or repression.**[2]

Bolivian diplomats have accused the Bush administration of conditioning economic and military assistance upon the involvement of the army in anti-narcotics activities.[3] In mid-1990, Bolivia's Vice President Luis Ossio Sanjines reported that U.S. Ambassador Robert Gelbard had explicitly told the government that aid to the army was contingent upon its role in the anti-drug struggle. More recently, the chair of the House Subcommittee on Western Hemisphere Affairs angrily questioned administration officials about reports that the U.S. embassy in Bolivia had pressured the Bolivian government to fire its ambassador to the United States. The U.S. pressure allegedly occurred because the ambassador had privately challenged the appropriateness of the administration's military aid program in meetings with members of Congress.[4]

Over the past few years, the U.S. has been particularly insistent on Bolivian cooperation. Bolivia has remained dependent on the international financial community and upon the United States. In early 1991, the United States temporarily suspended aid to Bolivia because of its non-cooperation with the United States in anti-narcotics activities. Although aid was restored, the Bolivian government continues to be pressured by Congress' linking U.S. support for loans from international development banks to cooperation in the drug war. Military and other government officials report that U.S.

---

[2] Samuel Doria Medina, Embassy of Bolivia, in hearings before the Senate Committee on the Judiciary and the Senate Caucus on International Narcotics Control, March 27, 1990, p. 7. (emphasis added)

[3] Christopher Marquis, "Bolivia to Use U.S. Drug Aid for Environment," The Miami Herald, September 11, 1990.

[4] Representative Robert Torricelli (D-NJ), "Review of the 1991 International Narcotics Control Strategy Report," op cit. pp. 78-79.

Ambassador Gelbard was especially vocal and persistent in urging counter-narcotics as a priority in-country.[5]

In May 1990, the Bolivian government signed a bilateral anti-narcotics accord with the United States that solidified the agreements reached in Cartagena four months earlier. In the face of intense U.S. pressure, a specific section on military aid ("Annex 3", reproduced in Appendix B) was included in which the Paz Zamora government agreed to expand military participation in the drug war, notably that of the army. Included in the accord are (1) for the Army, equipping and training two light-infantry Army battalions for anti-narcotics operations, and one engineer battalion for civic action; (2) for the Air Force, providing up to six UH-1H helicopters, reconditioning or repairing of up to thirty airplanes of various types, upgrading maintenance facilities, and joint testing of a mobile radar unit in the Chapare; and (3) for the Navy, equipping and training a Marine Infantry company for riverine operations, providing up to eleven patrol boats, including at least three more "Piranha"-class boats, and construction of a support facility for patrol boats and other ships.[6] In addition, the agreement permits U.S. assistance to be used for establishing a Counter-Narcotics Joint Operations Center, a Combined Joint Intelligence Center, a long-range communications network, a Public Information Section, medical and communications companies, and a Counter-Narcotics Training Center.

Even then, the Bolivian government held the army out of anti-narcotics operations for almost a year. The bilateral accord left the timing and exact details of army participation to Paz Zamora's discretion. Three months after its signing, the U.S. Embassy reportedly threatened to withhold aid to the army until participation in the drug war was forthcoming. In reaction against U.S. pressure, President Paz announced in September that drug-related U.S. military aid would be used to form military environmental protection patrols and an emergency reserve force.[7] Reports again surfaced that the U.S. would withhold the army's allotment of military aid until the army became involved in the drug war.[8]

Under continued U.S. pressure, the Bolivian government in early 1991 decided to permit army training and anti-drug operations. When it was officially acknowledged that U.S. trainers would soon arrive to begin training

---

[5] Various interviews. Ambassador Gelbard became Deputy Assistant Secretary of State for Central America in July 1991.

[6] See Annex III of Bolivia-U.S. bilateral counter-narcotics agreement, "Counter-Narcotics Program: Expanded Bolivian Armed Forces Participation," May 1990, pp. 3-7.

[7] Marquis, op cit.

[8] EFE Madrid, "U.S. Ties Aid to Army in Fight Against Drugs," in Foreign Broadcast Information Service, November 7, 1990, p. 33. See also Marquis, op cit.

army units, protests erupted from labor groups, opposition parties, and the Catholic church. This opposition -- rooted in nationalist sentiments and fears that militarization will strengthen military intervention in politics, fuel corruption, and spark political unrest, especially in the volatile coca-growing regions -- spanned parties from left to right.[9] The Bolivian Congress met in a special session and, only after a debate that lasted until almost midnight, agreed to authorize the presence of U.S. troops.[10] Five hours later, the first planeload of U.S. trainers, along with 90 tons of ammunition and equipment, arrived in La Paz.[11]

PERU

The Peruvian government has driven the hardest bargain with the United States, insisting that the economic component receive more attention and that the military aid package conform more to the Peruvian government's priorities. U.S. officials report that the Fujimori government's objections to the U.S. proposal for Peru were related to the uses and levels of economic aid.[12] The Peruvian armed forces have also resisted involvement in anti-narcotics activities, consistently pressing instead for aid to fight insurgencies.

An agreement was not reached in fiscal year 1990 between the United States and Peru, and $34.9 million in military assistance and $60 million in economic aid was foregone by the Fujimori government. Although it appeared that an agreement was near in September 1990, the Fujimori government decided that its interests were not sufficiently addressed. The military aid was reprogrammed to Peru's neighbors, with $30.9 million going to Colombia and $5.0 million to Bolivia.

In May 1991, the Peruvian and U.S. governments finally signed a bilateral umbrella agreement on anti-drug cooperation. The agreement, which is very general in nature and contains none of the details of U.S. economic or military assistance, was reportedly drafted mostly by Peruvians and

---

[9] See "Bolivians Resist U.S. Aid terms," Latinamerica Press, May 10, 1990, p. 7.

[10] Opposition leaders accused the governing coalition of violating parliamentary procedures to win the vote. See Radio Fides Transcript, April 3, 1991, in Foreign Broadcast Information Service, April 4, 1991, p. 17.

[11] Ibid., and James Painter, "Bolivians Protest US Militarization of Drug War," The Christian Science Monitor, April 15, 1991.

[12] U.S. officials' statements are from interviews and meetings with WOLA staff, 1990-91.

71

contained a number of concessions by the Bush administration.[13] The accord explicitly drew a distinction between peasant coca growers and drug traffickers:

> The coca-growing farmers constitute an economic and social class quite distinct from those individuals devoted to narcotics trafficking. The farmers are poor and engage in the activity primarily for subsistence reasons, because they cannot legally enter into another; the traffickers are prosperous and face no such barriers.[14]

In an unusual passage, the governments state that "this Agreement is intended to transcend the traditional type of cooperation between the United States and Peru in this area," depicting future cooperation as one of equal partners rather than as a unilateral "United States concern and responsibility in Peruvian territory."[15] Most importantly, in part by delaying until the second year of the Andean strategy, Peru will receive economic assistance simultaneously with military assistance.

The Bush administration also achieved some of its most important goals. The umbrella accord was followed in July 1991 by three separate bilateral accords governing economic, military and law enforcement assistance. With the signing of a military aid agreement, the U.S. effectively overcame the last barrier to involving every armed service in the three Andean Initiative countries in the drug war.[16] The agreement also allows the U.S. to attempt to realize its broader Andean ridge objectives in Peru, which include renewing ties with the Peruvian military and helping stabilize the government in the face of insurgencies.[17]

The military aid package also reflects some of the preferences of the Peruvian government. About one-third of the $34.9 million governed by the agreement in FY 1991 is slated for use in civic action programs designed to

---

[13] U.S. officials reported to WOLA that Peruvians drafted 90% of the umbrella agreement, and that the Instituto de Libertad y Democracia (Institute for Liberty and Democracy), directed by Peruvian economist Hernando De Soto, played a key role in the drafting of the accord on behalf of the Peruvian government.

[14] "An Agreement Between the United States of America and Peru on Drug Control and Alternative Development Policy," para. 9(b).

[15] Ibid., para. 7.

[16] U.S. officials reported to WOLA that the law enforcement agreement was agreed to very quickly, while the economic and military agreements required more negotiation. According to these officials, both the economic and military assistance agreements were drafted by the United States government.

[17] See "Andean Ridge Objectives," "SouthCom Southern Theatre Strategy."

foster goodwill with the local population in coca-growing areas.[18] This use was not listed as part of the proposed U.S. military aid package for Peru. Both governments agreed that only two of the initial six strike battalions would be trained with FY 1991 monies. And converging with the U.S. concept of the drug war in Peru, the accord responds to the Peruvians' interest in fighting Sendero Luminoso, explicitly sanctioning the use of anti-narcotics assistance for counterinsurgency.

COLOMBIA

The Colombian government has been the most open to U.S. military assistance for its police and armed forces. The Colombian government quickly agreed to a greater role for its armed forces in anti-narcotics in 1989. Since President Bush's offer of $65 million in emergency drawdown equipment in August 1989, the Colombian government has consistently accepted U.S. military aid for both police and military units, as well as U.S. trainers for Colombian police and military forces. The Colombian army, which has not put up the resistance to an anti-narcotics role offered by the Peruvian and Bolivian armies, has become more involved in anti-narcotics in the past year, although it remains secondary to the National Police in such efforts.

At the same time, the Colombian government has never viewed the military component of the Andean strategy as essential to its anti-narcotics objectives. In February 1991, Colombia's foreign minister said that Colombia was willing to forego both economic and military assistance if the United States would offer trade concessions.[19] Furthermore, the recent tensions between the U.S. and Colombian governments over the legal treatment of drug traffickers could signal trouble in what have been congenial relations. The Bush administration strongly opposed the decision of the recent Constituent Assembly to prohibit extradition, and members of the U.S. Congress have joined administration officials in expressing concerns that Pablo Escobar not be let off lightly.

To date, however, the two governments have cooperated quietly on military matters -- as indicated by the lack of much public information about the U.S. military's role in Colombia. Staff members of key U.S. congressional committees are unaware of the contents of bilateral military

---

[18] This information was provided by U.S. Ambassador to Peru, Anthony Quainton, in a meeting with WOLA staff in August 1991.

[19] Statement made on Radio Cadena Nacional, cited in "Colombia renuncia a ayuda económica de EE.UU.", Diario Las Américas, February 15, 1991.

anti-drug agreements between the U.S. and Colombian governments,[20] and U.S. officials are much more close-mouthed about operations in Colombia than in any other country. Congressional questioning of the Andean strategy is much less focused on Colombia than on Peru or Bolivia, possibly because of the widespread sentiment among the U.S. media and public against the Colombian cartels. The cartels' firepower and counterintelligence capabilities have contributed to a perceived need for secrecy about U.S. operations in that country. In addition, the U.S. has not engaged in highly public and controversial negotiations as is the case in Bolivia and Peru, the Colombian government and security forces have seen anti-narcotics as a higher priority than their Bolivian or Peruvian counterparts.

II. IMPLEMENTATION OF THE MILITARY COMPONENT OF THE ANDEAN STRATEGY

Since the beginning of the Andean strategy in the fall of 1989, the role of the United States armed forces has increased dramatically in "counter-narcotics" activities in the Andes. Marginal in such policy before 1989, the Department of Defense has become a principal actor in the formulation and implementation of the Andean strategy. U.S. troops are now planning and coordinating drug raids in Bolivia and Peru, which are carried out by U.S. DEA agents and Andean forces. The number of U.S. military personnel in the Andean region has multiplied to several hundred, and the range of authorized military activities has expanded to include everything short of participation in actual operations. DEA agents in the Bolivian jungle are now able to hook up to intelligence data banks in Washington, D.C., in two minutes. Allocated military assistance has jumped from less than $5 million in FY 1988 to $142 million in FY 1990. While U.S. training of armed forces has proceeded at different rates in each country, military training of police forces has been underway in each country since at least 1989. U.S. military officials report that the Persian Gulf War, which displaced significant amounts of equipment used in interdiction in the air and the sea, had little effect on security assistance programs "on the ground" in the Andean countries. And with the end of the Gulf war, the U.S. military has refocused attention on the drug war and is seeking to expand its anti-narcotics efforts throughout the hemisphere.

---

[20] Senior staff member of key House subcommittee. August 1991.

Increased U.S. Military Resources

The U.S. Southern Command in Panama was organized around the counter-drug mission in 1990, making the drug war the top priority in the hemisphere. SouthCom's anti-drug budget jumped from $230 million in FY 1990 to over $430 million in FY 1991.[21] The proposed FY 1992 anti-drug budget for the command is about $100 million, plus a requested $143 million for expansion of the Command Management System.[22] One SouthCom official reported that the command's anti-drug efforts "continue to be overwhelmingly focused on Colombia, Bolivia and Peru," even while they are being expanded to the Tier II and Tier III countries in the rest of the hemisphere.[23] The number of military personnel devoted to anti-drug activities has increased sharply since the Panama invasion, and SouthCom officials report that the drug war remains the command's top military mission[24] The Command set up a Counter-narcotics Center in 1989 which is staffed by about 30 officers.

Levels of Security Assistance

The level of operational support given Andean countries by the U.S. military has skyrocketed since 1988 (see Table 4.A). The bulk of that support is provided through security assistance programs of the U.S. government.[25] Military assistance to Colombia, Peru, and Bolivia totalled less

---

[21] Remarks of Col. Larry Izzo, Joint Staff, DOD Press Briefing, March 9, 1990.

[22] "The Widening Drug War," Newsweek, July 1, 1991.

[23] Personal Interview, August 1991.

[24] Personal interviews with Southern Command official and with well-informed Washington analysts, mid-1991.

[25] Many U.S. military activities in the Andes (e.g., Deployments-for-Training teams, some Mobile Training Teams, intelligence equipment which remains in the hands of the United States, intelligence-gathering cooperation activities) can be funded directly through the Department of Defense's annual budget (authorized by the House and Senate Armed Services Committees), rather than through the foreign assistance budget (authorized by the House Foreign Affairs and the Senate Foreign Relations Committees). SouthCom's budget, for example, is appropriated through the Defense Department appropriations. In addition, the activities of the CIA are funded through the CIA's classified budget (authorized by the Intelligence Committees in both houses), which may also be used for activities of any military (or other) personnel assigned to the CIA. Foreign assistance (including all security and economic aid) plus the State Department's narcotics-related support activities, are funded through the foreign aid appropriations process every one or two years.

There is disagreement over the definitions of "security assistance" and "military assistance" within the U.S. government. Some agencies do not include Economic Support Funds in security assistance figures, and some agencies do not include 506 drawdown equipment in military assistance totals. The usage of "security assistance" here conforms to that of the Office of Management and Budget and the Foreign Assistance Act of 1961: "security assistance" includes "military assistance" as well as other security-related programs such as Economic Support Funds (ESF), anti-terrorism assistance (ATA), and aid for peace-keeping operations. And the usage of "military assistance" here conforms to that of Chart 4.A, provided by the House Committee on Foreign Affairs: "military assistance" includes foreign military financing (FMF), international military education and training (IMET), and military equipment drawdown from existing stocks under Sections 506(a) and 506(b) of the Foreign Assistance Act of 1961.

Table 4.A
NARCOTICS-RELATED U.S. ASSISTANCE TO THE ANDES
(in millions of dollars)

COLOMBIA

	FY 1989 Actual	FY 1990 Request	FY 1990 Actual	FY 1991 Request	FY 1991 Allocated	FY 1992 Request
FMF	7.1	40.0	71.7	58.0	27.0	58.0
506 drawdown	65.0	0.0	20.0	-	?	?
IMET	1.0	1.5	1.5	2.5	2.5	2.3
EDA	0.0	0.0	0.0	0.0	3.0	0.0
Military Total	73.1	41.5	93.2	60.5	32.5	60.3
ESF	2.8	0.0	2.1	50.0	50.0	50.0
INM	10.0	20.0	20.0	20.0	20.0	20.0
TOTAL:	85.9	61.5	115.3	130.5	102.5	130.3

BOLIVIA

	FY 1989 Actual	FY 1990 Request	FY 1990 Actual	FY 1991 Request	FY 1991 Allocated	FY 1992 Request
FMF	5.0	33.0	39.2	40.0	35.0	40.0
506 drawdown	0.0	0.0	7.8	-	-	-
IMET	.4	.5	.5	.9	.9	.9
Military Total	5.4	33.5	47.5	40.9	35.9	40.9
ESF	25.0	30.0	33.4	95.8	77.0	125.0
DA	11.7	31.9	24.2	23.5	22.5	22.5
INM	10.0	15.7	15.7	15.7	15.7	15.7
TOTAL:	52.1	111.1	120.8	175.9	151.1	204.1

PERU

	FY 1989 Actual	FY 1990 Request	FY 1990 Actual	FY 1991 Request	FY 1991 Allocated	FY 1992 Request
FMF	2.5	36.4	1.0	39.0	34.0	39.0
IMET	.5	.5	.5	.9	.9	.9
Military Total	3.0	36.9	1.5	39.9	34.9	39.9
ESF	2.0	5.0	3.2	63.1	60.0	100.0
DA	17.8	24.1	16.0	11.8	9.7	15.7
INM	10.5	10.0	10.0	19.0	19.0	19.0
TOTAL:	33.3	76.0	30.7	133.8	123.6	174.6

	FY 1989 Actual	FY 1990 Request	FY 1990 Actual	FY 1991 Request	FY 1991 Allocated	FY 1992 Request
Total Military:	81.5	111.2	142.2	141.3	103.3	141.1
Total Economic:	59.3	91.0	78.9	244.2	221.3	313.2
Total INM:	30.5	45.7	45.7	54.7	54.7	54.7

Notes for Table 4.A

a. In addition to economic aid in the chart, Bolivia and Peru also receive about $60-100 million per year combined in food aid.
b. In addition to funds listed above for law enforcement, INM spends about $25 million per year for air support to the Andean countries.
c. In addition to funds listed for FY 1990 law enforcement, each country received $1 million in FMF for weapons/ammunition; and Colombia received an additional $1 million for defensive arming of drug control aircraft.
d. Fiscal year 1991 and 1992 totals do not include further possible assistance out of other military assistance spigots (EDA/506(a)).
e. For fiscal year 1992, INM support to Peru will be funded out of its Latin American regional account.
f. For fiscal year 1991, $175 million was specifically set aside for the Andes; for fiscal year 1992, $250 million was so specified. Fiscal year 1992 ESF requests by country are still under discussion.

SOURCE (table and notes): House Foreign Affairs Committee, 1991.

than $5 million in fiscal year 1988. In FY 1989, military aid jumped to $73.1 million, including $65 million "drawdown" from U.S. defense stocks for Colombia immediately after the assassination of presidential candidate Luis Carlos Galán in August 1989.

In FY 1990, military aid allocated to these three countries exceeded $142 million -- more than the military assistance received by all of Central America that year and a twenty-fold increase over a two-year period. In that year, Colombia has been allocated received $93.2 million in military aid, including $20 million in drawndown equipment, surpassing El Salvador as the top military aid recipient in the hemisphere. Bolivia's military aid total jumped from $5.4 million in FY 1989 to over $47 million in 1990, when it signed the military aid agreement with the United States.[26]

In FY 1992, the administration has requested from Congress over $416 million in security assistance, including ESF, to Colombia, Bolivia, and Peru, the highest for that region in history.[27] Peru is slated to receive $34.9 million in military aid and $60 million in ESF in FY 1991, both unprecedented figures which together are over three times more than Peru has ever received from the United States in security assistance.[28] The administration's request for $39.9 million in military aid for FY 1992 would be the most ever given to that country by the United States.

Indeed, Colombia, Bolivia and Peru are slated to receive more military assistance than all of Central America over the three-year period between FY 1990 and FY 1992. Even if drawdown equipment is excluded, the Andean total of $349 million for that period exceeds the total for the seven-country Central American isthmus by almost $20 million.[29]

As stated earlier, congressional sources report that the vast majority of Foreign Military Financing under the Andean strategy for FY 1990 and FY

---

[26] As mentioned earlier, Peru's allocation of $35.9 million in military assistance for FY 1990 was turned down and reprogrammed to Colombia ($30.9 million -- included in totals in Table 4.A) and Bolivia ($5 million).

[27] Calculations based on "U.S. Bilateral Economic and Military Assistance to Latin America and the Caribbean, Fiscal Years 1946 to 1987," by K. Larry Storrs, for the Congressional Research Service, July 1987, as well as on other figures provided by the Congressional Research Service and on Chart 4.A.

[28] The most U.S. military assistance Peru has ever received was $21.32 million in FY 1975, and the most security assistance ever delivered to Peru was $26.9 million in FY 1962. Storrs, ibid., p. 34.

[29] These figures are based on calculations from figures of the House Foreign Affairs Committee (actual obligations for FY 1990, estimated obligations for FY 1991, and the administration's requests for FY 1992). The total for the three Andean countries excludes $7 million which at the time of this writing appeared to be withheld from FMF to Peru for FY 1991.

1991 has not been delivered.[30]   However, because "drawdown" equipment must be delivered within a specified time frame, approximately $3.8 million of it has arrived in Colombia in the two years since the first $65 million was delivered in FY 1989 (see Table 4.B).   Indeed, the Defense Department is using a wide variety of mechanisms for authorizing the deliveries, including emergency drawdown authority (Sec. 506(a)(1) Foreign Assistance Act), drug-related drawdown authority (506(a)(2) drawdown authority), authority for modernization military forces for anti-narcotics (Sec. 517, Foreign Assistance Act), and transfer to foreign governments of confiscated equipment seized in US drug operations (Sec. 4501, Anti-Drug Abuse Act).   While the Congress has an opportunity to express its opposition to the delivery of most of these items, these deliveries are not part of the annual legislative budget process, and represent additions to annual administration assistance request totals.

Planning and Coordination of Anti-narcotics Operations
After 1988, Tactical Analysis Teams (TATs) were established in Bolivia, Peru, and Colombia as key components of SouthCom's advisory function. Made up of a small number of U.S. Special Forces and military intelligence personnel, TATs draw together intelligence to select targets and plan drug raids to be carried out by Andean police and military forces and DEA agents.[31]   National forces of the Andean countries are not part of TATs.   In addition, SouthCom reports that two Special Forces personnel are deployed to each of Colombia's fourteen regional police headquarters in an advisory capacity.[32]

The TATs, in conjunction with the DEA and with SouthCom personnel stationed in Panama, play the lead role in the planning and coordinating major anti-narcotics operations in Bolivia, and play a similar role in Peru.   The two highest profile drug raids to date in Bolivia illustrate the U.S. military's central role.   In September 1990, the Tactical Analysis Team in Bolivia used intelligence that had been drawn from both human sources and technical resources to plan a raid on a cocaine plant run by Bolivian Carmelo Meco Domínguez, accused of being a major drug trafficker.   Based on SouthCom officers' accounts, Newsweek described the planning:

---

[30] On August 21, 1991, Gen. Joulwan formally delivered eighteen OV-10 airplanes (which had arrived July 22) to the Colombian Air Force.   Colombian military sources stated that the airplanes would be used for counterinsurgency.   "Se incrementa la Fuerza Aérea colombiana con 18 aviones de EEUU," El Universal, Mexico, August 22, 1991, p. 2.

[31] "Stopping the Flood...," op cit., p. 52.   Also "The Widening Drug War," Newsweek, July 1, 1991.

[32] Interview with Col. Robert Jacobelly, commander of the advisory teams, early 1991, Quarry Heights, Panama.

"The tactical-analysis team, working through DEA agents and Bolivian police, spent months watching the organization covertly. Agents photographed gang members and their smuggling planes; nine planes were seized in the raid. It also used satellite reconnaissance, offshore radar surveillance and ground sensors to trace the gang's smuggling patterns."[33]

On September 24, about 300 Bolivian police agents and 20 DEA agents raided a major cocaine-producing plant in the Chapare region. Meco Domínguez and about 70 others were arrested, of which the DEA claims about 17 were active in cocaine production and trafficking.[34]

In June 1991, the U.S. military again played a key role in planning and coordinating a large-scale raid as part of an operation called, "Safehaven."[35] Drawing on the plans prepared by the tactical analysis team, about 580 Bolivian police and 33 DEA agents took control of the town of Santa Ana del Yacuma. The operation resulted in 54 arrests, 15 cocaine base and HCl laboratories destroyed, 40 aircraft seized, 9 estates seized, and 110 kilos of cocaine base.[36] A senior U.S. anti-narcotics official called it the "largest and most complex paramilitary operation the DEA has ever undertaken anywhere in the world."[37] Although the raid failed to net the targeted drug traffickers, DEA officials claim that the operation prompted Bolivia's largest traffickers to begin negotiations with the government for surrender. The operation involved demobilizing the military outpost in the town, which was viewed as complicit in drug trafficking.[38]

Following the raid, Bolivian officials publicly complained about the U.S.' role in controlling intelligence and in carrying out anti-narcotics operations in that country. Referring to U.S. officials, a senior aide to President Paz Zamora said, "They know more than we do -- for instance, where the cocainelaboratories are -- and sometimes they don't even share the information with us."[39] Bolivian officials also stated that the DEA did more than "accompany" Bolivian police in the Santa Ana raid, and in the future "to closely enforce the terms of our bilateral agreement, which says DEA agents

---

[33] "The Widening Drug War," op cit., p. 33.

[34] See "The Widening Drug War," op cit., and testimony of Charles Gutensohn, then-Chief, Cocaine Investigations Section, DEA, before the Task Force on International Narcotics Matters of the House Foreign Affairs Committee, July 10, 1991, p. 9.

[35] Sam Dillon, "Bolivia to Cut U.S. Role in Drug War," The Miami Herald, July 1991, p. 1A.

[36] Testimony by Gutensohn, DEA, op cit.

[37] Ibid.

[38] Dillon, op cit.

[39] Dillon, op cit.

Table 4.B
U.S. ASSISTANCE TO COLOMBIA, FY 1990-1991:
PROVIDED ADDITIONAL TO ANNUAL MILITARY AID REQUESTS
(Outside of FMF, IMET Accounts)

August 19, 1990	Estimated Current $US Value
(Under Sec 506(b), Foreign Assistance Act)	
COLOMBIAN NATIONAL POLICE	
Troop support equipment	3,991
UH-1H Support	571,927
COLOMBIAN AIR FORCE	
Communications support	201,159
Aviator equipment	54,050
C-130B aircraft	1,785,390
Ferry of C-130B	25,000
Aviation support items	117,318
C-130 spare parts	52,989
Miscellaneous aircraft spare parts	83,994
Mobile Training Teams	168,700
May 10, 1991	
(Under Sec. 517, Foreign Assistance Act)	
Ten civilian vehicles (vans, carry-alls, etc.)	70,000 (up to 140,000)
July 5, 1991	
(Under Sec. 4501, Anti-Drug Abuse Act)	
J69 Engines	70,108
July 5, 1991	
(Under Sec. 519, Foreign Assistance Act)	
Excess support equipment for OV-10 aircraft	35,612
July 15, 1991	
(Under Sec. 517, Foreign Assistance Act)	
Four Landing Craft ships	571,000
July 18, 1991	
(Under Sec. 517, Foreign Assistance Act)	
Further excess support equipment for OV-10 aircraft	16,276
TOTAL, FY 1990-FY 1991 (@ JULY 1991)	**$3,827,514**

Sources: Letters of notification from Lt. Gen. Teddy Allen, Defense Security Assistance Agency to House Committee on Foreign Affairs. For May 1991 delivery, letter from Janet Mullins, State Department, to House Committee on Foreign Affairs. After July 5, 1991, letters from Glenn Rudd, Defense Security Assistance Agency to House Committee on Foreign Affairs.

cannot participate in operations."[40]   The commander-in-chief of the armedforces, Gen. Jorge Moreira, called alleged DEA abuses of a Bolivian navy official during the raid an "affront" to the Bolivian military, called for the expulsion of those involved, and investigations were initiated.[41]   The Bolivian officials' statements indicate that the U.S. military's planning role and the DEA's operational role were decisive in the Santa Ana raid.

Intelligence Support

Since 1989, SouthCom has focused intense efforts at increasing intelligence-gathering capabilities, denying such capabilities to drug traffickers, and coordinating intelligence efforts with Andean forces. Little information is presently available about the nature of coordination of intelligence efforts with the police or military forces of any of the Andean countries. However, overall intelligence-gathering programs have proceeded steadily. Dozens of operations involving particular technological applications have been initiated, with names such as Operation Snow Find, Operation Snow Ear, and Operation Snow Eagle. Intelligence-gathering efforts now involve communications between a host of components -- AWACs and E2-C airplanes, the Caribbean Basin Radar Network, airplanes overflying Andean countries, Navy ships in the Caribbean, and intelligence centers in Panama, in El Paso, Texas, and in other places in the United States.[42]

SouthCom's pilot program of the Command Management System in Bolivia is now operational. DEA and other agents in the field can take a color photograph of a plane or trafficker with a digitalized camera that contains a computer disk, place the disk in a mobile or fixed computer unit, transmit the information through satellite to the Counter-narcotics Operations Center in Panama and to Washington, D.C., all within about 120 seconds.[43] Phone conversations by drug traffickers can also be intercepted with high-tech equipment, and Air Force and Army planes fly out of Howard Air Force Base in Panama on reconnaissance flights.[44] Many of the Caribbean Basin Radar Network's fixed radars are now operational, and mobile radars operated off ships and in the air are also being utilized. In Colombia, the two ship-based mobile radar that were removed for the Persian Gulf War are now

---

[40] Ibid.

[41] James Painter, "Bolivian Military Leader Questions DEA's Role in Drug Bust Gone Awry," The Christian Science Monitor, July 12, 1991, and Dillon, ibid.

[42] SouthCom Strategy documents, late 1990, and "The Widening Drug War," op cit.

[43] Information provided by a SouthCom official, August 1991.

[44] Laura Brooks, "US Military Extends Drug War Into Central America," Christian Science Monitor, June 25, 1991.

back in place and operational.[45] In addition, three army ships equipped with aerostat radar balloons run regular patrols out of Panama in the Caribbean.[46] SouthCom officials report that they have made progress in Congress and within the administration in getting the funds for expanding the Command Management System in Central America and in other regions within South America.[47]

In Colombia, the press and some government officials have accused the United States Air Force of carelessness and unauthorized flight patterns -- which have led to near-accidents -- during U.S. air surveillance activities. In August 1991, the Colombian Civil Aeronautics Board also declared that U.S. airplanes have carried out "irregular" flights in "intelligence" missions, especially in the area around the prison where Pablo Escobar and his associates are currently imprisoned.[48] The Board recognized that U.S. planes have permission to fly between Howard Air Force Base in Panama and Colombia's Palanquero air base, but sanctioned a U.S. pilot who flew over an unauthorized area near Medellín. The U.S. Air Force Caza 212, flying about 4,000 feet below the authorized minimum height of 14,000 feet for that area, nearly collided with a Colombian Avianca jetliner near the jail holding Escobar.[49] An air traffic controller told the Avianca captain, "This is not the first time we have been on the edge of tragedy. The Casa airplane is a DEA airplane, and during the past three weeks it has infringed on all of our security norms."[50] The incident followed another reported near-collision in March 1990 between a U.S. Air Foce C-130 and an Avianca passenger jet. Other incidents of unauthorized U.S. flights have been reported. The Colombian press and some politicians have criticized the U.S. flights, and the office of Colombia's Attorney-General is investigating the incidents.

Training

Since 1987, U.S. military forces have trained over a thousand Andean personnel. SouthCom officials believe that training efforts, carried out by U.S. Army, Navy, Air Force and Marines, are critical to improved Andean police and military capabilities.

---

[45] Personal interview, SouthCom officials, mid-1991.

[46] Laura Brooks, op cit.

[47] Ibid. SouthCom hopes to place one fixed CMS computer console in a U.S. Embassy in the Central American region, another in the Northern portion of South America, and one in Argentina or Uruguay.

[48] "Aerocivil sanciona a piloto de EE.UU. que violó espacio aéreo," La Prensa, August 29, 1991.

[49] "Objetos Voladores DEA-ntificados," La Prensa, August 25, 1991.

[50] Quoted in Leslie Wirpsa, "U.S. Coalition Calls on Bush to Redirect Drug-War Dollars," National Catholic Reporter, September 13, 1991.

BOLIVIA

Between April 1987 and 1991, U.S. Special Forces Mobile Training Teams (MTTs) conducted Operation Red Dragon, the first narcotics-related military training program for foreign forces in the Andes. During that time, over 1,000 ground police of the UMOPAR (Unidad Movil de Patrullaje Rural) anti-narcotics force were trained at a police base in Chimore. To date, UMOPAR ground forces (known as the "Leopards") have received the bulk of U.S. police training in the Andean region.

As of early 1991, Operation Red Dragon was being phased out and replaced by a new operation known as Operation Stone Bridge.[51] Training of UMOPAR forces continues, but it is conducted by Bolivian trainers who are monitored by U.S. Special Forces. Operation Stone Bridge is aimed at providing advice and assistance to the DEA and to UMOPAR forces in carrying out anti-drug raids. Selected UMOPAR officers also receive specialized training from U.S. Rangers at Ft. Benning, Georgia. Records from the U.S. Army School of the Americas indicate that 81 Bolivian police and military personnel received trained there in 1990 with funding provided by the State Department's INM (see Chart 4.C).[52] That training consisted not only of counter-narcotics courses, but also standard infantry, military intelligence and strategic military intelligence, psychological operations, and commando courses.

In addition to ongoing police training, the U.S. military has trained Bolivian military personnel since 1988. Navy SEALs (Sea, Land, and Air) units continue to train riverine forces (known as "Blue Devils") drawn from the Bolivian Navy. The riverine unit numbered fifty in 1988. And the "Red Devils," a 12-helicopter air wing drawn from the Bolivian Air Force, received training from an Army warrant officer on loan to the State Department. The airwing numbered sixty persons at the end of 1988.[53]

In May 1991, U.S. Special Forces trainers arrived in Bolivia to begin training the units of the national army as part of a U.S.-Bolivian bilateral agreement signed in May 1990. The training, known as Operation White Spear, consists of two ten-week sessions involving 56 Green berets each. Bolivian army officials report that around 2,000 -- or a little less than one-tenth of the Bolivian army -- will be trained. Under the accord, which

---

[51] The information in this paragraph is from personal interviews with SOUTHCOM officials.

[52] Close Out Reports, "INM Projections," U.S. Army School of the Americas, 1990.

[53] "Stopping the Flood...," op cit., p. 49; and Thirty-eighth Report, p. 72.

SouthCom officials confirm will guide their training, two Light Infantry battalions will be trained for counter-narcotics operations, one engineering battalion for civic action, and one transportation company and one Supply and Service section for operational support. The training will occur at Montero, a Bolivian Ranger base about 60 miles north of Santa Cruz built by the U.S. in the 1960s.[54]

The agreement also mandated an increased role for the Bolivian Air Force and Navy in counter-narcotics. Under the new accord, the Navy will receive training and equipment for a Marine Infantry Company and for a Supply and Service section. The Air Force would receive training and equipment for an Air Military Police unit and for a Supply and Service section. The training of these Air Force and Navy units has already begun.[55]

PERU

In "Operation Blue Venture," U.S. Special Forces Mobile Training Teams have trained Peruvian anti-narcotics and counterinsurgency police units since April 1989. State Department officials report that 90% of these units have been anti-narcotics (DIPOD) units, and that 10% have been police agents of the counter-insurgency unit known as the "Sinchis". The training has been conducted at the Sinchis' Mazamari camp in central Peru.

Of the three Andean Initiative countries, only the armed forces of Peru have not received narcotics-related training from the U.S. military. However, with the bilateral anti-narcotics accord, training will soon begin. Following Peru's signing of the accord, U.S. officials announced that groups of U.S. military trainers would be sent to Peru to advise the Peruvian armed forces in anti-narcotics and counterinsurgency operations.[56] Administration officials did not give exact numbers, but said that more than 50 advisers at a time would be operating in Peru. These trainers will include U.S. Army Green Berets and Navy personnel. Each of the two combat units trained by Special Forces would be assigned a group of 25 trainers, according to the officials. The Navy units would be assigned to train Peruvian riverine patrols, and "an unspecified number of military would be assigned to human rights training."

---

[54] Thirty-eighth Report, p. 74.

[55] Personal interview with U.S. government analyst.

[56] The information in this paragraph is from Clifford Krauss, "U.S. Military Team to Advise Peru in War Against Drugs and Rebels," The New York Times, August 7, 1991.

COLOMBIA

The U.S. military has provided training and logistical support to the Colombian military for several years. Between 1987 and 1990, over 2,000 Colombian military personnel were trained at the U.S. Army School of the Americas in Georgia (see Appendix D). During that time, Colombia accounted for 37% of all students, and no country (including El Salvador) had more trainees.[57]

U.S. Special Forces engage in two types of narcotics-related training operations in Colombia.[58] First, Special Forces "Aid Attachments" train Colombian "cadre" in six-week courses of about 40 students each. The intention is to train trainers ("cadre") who will train other Colombian troops.

Second, Special Forces Mobile Training Teams train police and military forces in basic soldiering skills and in equipment use. Presently the training program includes five levels: enlisted men (basic soldiering skills), squad leaders, Company commanders, Battalion commanders, and cadre to train others. SouthCom officials report that no strike battalions per se have been trained in Colombia, although such training may yet be given.

Substantial shipments of equipment to the Colombian military and police have been accompanied by parallel training in its use and maintenance. For example, when $65 million of equipment was drawn down from DOD stocks for Colombia in September 1989, of 38 troops reported to be working on anti-narcotics activities, 25 were associated with equipment delivery or maintenance.[59]

There is little information on U.S. Navy or Air Force training in Colombia. U.S. Air Force personnel have participated in training Colombian forces in the use of aircraft and air support and maintenance equipment provided by the United States under drawdown authority (see Tables 1.B, 4.B). In 1989, Marine units were reported to be training Colombian riverine units near the Peru-Colombia border.[60] In May 1991, Lt. Col. Joseph Rogish of the U.S. Marine Corps Combat Development Center reported that U.S.

---

[57] Of the 402 Colombian military personnel enrolled in courses in 1990, only two (2) were enrolled in a special counter-narcotics course begun that year.

[58] Again, this account does not include classified missions in Colombia, which military and non-military analysts acknowledge are taking place.

[59] Arms Control and Foreign Policy Caucus, November 1989, p. 3.

[60] Army Times, October 2, 1989.

Marine Mobile Training Teams were engaged in training Colombian forces in riverine operations in that country.[61]

Civic Action

In addition, civic action missions are conducted as part of U.S. anti-drug efforts in the Andes. Information on these missions is scant. These missions often draw on reserve forces, sent on "deployments-for-training," missions undertaken specifically for their training value to the U.S. troops.

U.S. Troop Levels in the Region

While the total number of U.S. troops in the Andes remains less than a few hundred, this number represents a sharp increase from previous years. Although the total number of U.S. military personnel in the region is classified, press accounts indicate that the number of troops in the Andes rose through 1990 and early 1991. In November 1989, the State Department reported that, of a total of 130-140 U.S. military personnel in Andean-Initiative countries, about 78 were engaged in drug-related efforts.[62] At the time, a senior administration official said that totals could reach "several hundred."[63] The Los Angeles Times reported that as many as 30-50 troops would be added to each country in the latter part of 1990.[64] That addition would bring U.S. troop totals in Colombia, Peru, and Bolivia, for unclassified missions, to between 200 and 300. With the recent initiation of Operation White Spear in Bolivia (involving 56 trainers at one time) and once training programs commence in Peru (involving over 50 trainers at a time), U.S. troops in the three countries as of mid-1991 would total between 300 and 400, not counting personnel for civic action programs and for other possible operations.

The Impact of the Persian Gulf War

Operationally, the Persian Gulf War displaced significant amounts of equipment used in air and sea interdiction in the Caribbean and Latin America. Most of the AWACS airplanes, which carry a mounted radar used to track aircraft over land and over the sea, were removed for use in the Gulf

---

[61] Quoted in notes from "Special Operations, Low Intensity Conflict and Drug Interdiction Conference," Conference organized by Technical Marketing Corporation of America, Washington, D.C., May 13-14, 1991.

[62] House Arms Control and Foreign Policy Caucus, "U.S. Military Involvement in the War on Drugs in Latin America," p. 3.

[63] The Washington Post, Sept. 13, 1989.

[64] Douglas Jehl, "GIs Escalate Attack on Drugs in S. America," The Los Angeles Times, July 2, 1990.

war. Col. Keith Nightingale, SouthCom's Counter-narcotics Chief said, "We're not playing with the same [numbers of] AWACs, boats, etc." He stated that the interdiction operations were significantly hampered by the displacement: "When the AWACs went to the Middle East, 'detection and monitoring' went with them."[65] Colombian government officials complained that two mobile radars, which SouthCom officials told WOLA were mounted on ships, were removed for use in the Persian Gulf.[66]

While the Gulf war significantly cut into the high-tech military "assets" used for interdiction, it had less effect on U.S. security assistance allocations and on programs "on the ground" in the Andean countries. Security assistance allocations continued to rise, although delivery was delayed for a variety of reasons.[67] SouthCom and DOD officials report that the Gulf War did not significantly affect training programs, civic action missions, or delivery of equipment. SouthCom's counter-narcotics chief indicates that limits placed on personnel levels worked to the advantage of anti-drug programs, maintaining previous personnel levels.[68]

As of mid-1991, many of the air and sea assets displaced to the Persian Gulf were back in use in the drug war in Latin America. SouthCom officials report that AWACs and E-2C overflights have resumed over the Andean region and the Caribbean.[69] SouthCom officials also report that the two ship-based mobile radar transferred to the Persian Gulf War are now back in place off the Colombian coast.[70] Perhaps more significantly, the administration has refocused some of its attention on the drug war, successfully obtaining a series of accords with the Peruvian government and initiating a military role in that country. One SouthCom official told WOLA that in the spring and summer of 1991, military and paramilitary operations in that country had increased in number, even after the surrender of Pablo Escobar.[71]

---

[65] Personal Interview, Quarry Heights, Panama, February 1991 (after the air strikes had begun in the Persian Gulf, but before the ground attack commenced).

[66] Cited by Douglas Farah, The Washington Post. Interviews with SouthCom official, mid-1991.

[67] Some members of Congress berated the administration for not having used all of the monies allocated in FY 1989 and FY 1990, although one senior committee staff member reported that it takes two to three years to get a new security assistance program in place. See House Foreign Affairs Committee, Report accompanying the International Cooperation Act of 1991, June 20, 1991; and, interview with staff member of House Foreign Affairs Committee, July 1991. These reasons were unrelated to the Persian Gulf War.

[68] WOLA interview, with Col. Keith Nightingale, Head of Counter-narcotics Center, SouthCom, early 1991.

[69] Interviews, mid-1991, and "The Widening Drug War," op cit.

[70] Personal interview, mid-1991.

[71] Ibid.

III. THE FUTURE OF THE U.S. MILITARY'S COUNTER-NARCOTICS ROLE

In its commitment to the multi-year counter-narcotics mission, the U.S. Southern Command is actively expanding and intensifying a range of programs, as reported in U.S. media.[72] U.S. military officials reported, "We've been attacking the Andean ridge. Now we're extending this war to transit areas."[73] According to one report, "The military is intensifying drug interdiction and intelligence gathering on land, sea, and air around the nations through which cocaine still flows to the U.S." SouthCom officials confirmed that it is attempting to implement initial programs in the Tier II and Tier III countries, including "discussions" with Central American countries.[74] Central American activities focus on Guatemala, which is increasingly used as a transit point and where production of poppies used for heroin has increased. In 1991 the DEA launched a program identical to Operation Snowcap in Guatemala, in which U.S. agents work with the Guatemala's G-2, military intelligence.[75] In addition, the State Department has overseen the drafting of an "overall Surrounding and Transit Country Strategy," and plans to use a small sum in Latin American Regional funds for "Central America, the Caribbean, and South America."[76] The significance of drug trafficking, as well as the problems an increased military role may bring, differs from country, and further information is needed on each. However, each of the country's exhibits increased military involvement, with U.S. support, in the drug war.

"Tier II" Countries

* In **ECUADOR**, primarily a transit country, the army has played an increasing role in anti-narcotics operations, launching regular border patrols and ground patrols. In late 1990, the Ecuadoran Congress passed an anti-drug law which formalized the role of the army in counter-narcotics efforts. Recently the U.S. government provided 470 vehicles for anti-drug operations, and in 1991 was slated to assist in the "development of an integrated counter-

---

[72] These included "U.S. Military Extends Drug War into Central America," The Christian Science Monitor, June 25; "The Widening Drug War," Newsweek, July 1; and a three-part series in The Miami Herald, July 1991.

[73] Laura Brooks, "U.S. Military Extends Drug War..." ibid.

[74] Ibid., and personal interviews, mid-1991.

[75] Interview with Charles Gutensohn, DEA, op cit.

[76] Assistant Secretary of State Levitsky, Testimony March 19, 1991, op cit., p. 7.

narcotics training program for Police and Army units involved in drug control." In 1991, the State Department said, "In Ecuador, we will help... support army counter-narcotics operations, increase military cooperation with the police in border areas, and expand Customs Police marine coastal patrols..."

* In support of law enforcement agencies, the **VENEZUELAN** army participated for the first time in cannabis eradication in late 1990.[77] U.S. Mobile Training Teams helped repair aircraft for anti-narcotics operations, and the Bush administration reported that it would provide more troops to repair helicopters in order to augment Venezuelan military involvement in drug control.[78]

* In addition to a series of increased law enforcement activities in **ARGENTINA**, the U.S. Southern Command participated in 1990 in a surveillance-interdiction exercise coordinated by the Argentine Air Force.[79] U.S. Special Forces reportedly carried out joint exercises with Argentinean armed forces in anti-narcotics operations in 1990,[80] and the United States is pressing the Argentinean air force to increase surveillance, despite constitutional prohibitions introduced following the military dictatorship regarding internal security missions for the armed forces.

* **BRAZIL**'s position as a key transshipment point has generated increasing concern among U.S. and other anti-narcotics officials. The State Department has pledged to provide "vehicles, boats, communications equipment, narcotics screening equipment and test kits, and operating costs to the National Police and Customs."[81] SouthCom's Special Forces Commander Robert Jacobelly told WOLA that Brazil had thus far turned down SouthCom's offer to train anti-drug military units.[82] Senator Alan Cranston (D-CA) expressed his concern over the Brazil military's involvement in the drug war:

"The [Bush] administration appears to be pushing the idea, as they have in other South American countries, that the Brazilian military ought to take a more active counter-narcotics role. The military, for its part, have sought to escape such a function, arguing

---

[77] 1991 INCSR, p. 125.

[78] Ibid.

[79] Ibid., p. 76.

[80] "Argentina: U.S. Green Berets move South," Latinamerica Press, May 31, 1990, p. 3.

[81] Assistant Secretary of State Melvyn Levitsky, in testimony March 19, 1991, op cit., p. 7.

[82] Personal interview, op cit.

that -- under Brazil's constitution -- anti-narcotics police form part of the Federal Police's function."[83]

* In June 1990, **PARAGUAY** formed a joint police-military task force, which began operations after receiving training from U.S. military personnel.[84]

"Tier III" Countries

* In **GUATEMALA**, cocaine trans-shipments increased sharply in 1990, and poppy cultivation grew by almost 30%, although U.S. officials report that more than half was eradicated through aerial and manual operations that year.[85]   In 1990, several U.S. newspapers reported that U.S. officials had changed their stance from opposing Guatemalan army participation in the drug war to believing that such participation was necessary.[86]

The U.S. reportedly has been paying members of Guatemalan military intelligence (known as S-2 or more commonly by its former initials G-2) for information, despite the agency's notoriety for identifying, abducting and killing suspected guerrilla sympathizers.   One U.S. drug expert was quoted as saying, "as long as they [G-2] keep doing good work, you don't ask about involvement in the killings and disappearances so often attributed to them."[87]   While both the CIA and the DEA are said to maintain regular contact with the G-2, U.S. officials vehemently deny that the G-2 has a major role in anti-narcotics operations.[88]

* Authorities in **COSTA RICA** estimated in mid-1991 that 2,000 kilos of cocaine pass through the country each month.[89]   In 1985,

---

[83] Remarks by Sen. Alan Cranston, Congressional Record, June 18, 1991, p. S8048. Sen. Cranston concluded, "On balance, and keeping in mind the horrible precedents being set by military involvement in places like Bolivia and Colombia, I think the Brazilian position is the more correct one."

[84] 1991 INCSR, p. 110.

[85] 1991 INCSR.

[86] Colum Lynch, "U.S.: Guatemala Army Must Fight Drug War," The Miami Herald, April 26, 1990; Lindsey Gruson, "U.S. Pins Hopes on Guatemalan Army," The New York Times, July 5, 1990; Kenneth Fried, "U.S. Is Taking new Tack in Guatemala," The Los Angeles Times, May 7, 1990.

[87] Fried, The Los Angeles Times, op cit.

[88] See WOLA, "Guatemala: A Test Case for Human Rights Policy in the Post-Cold War Era," 1991.

[89] Latin America News Update, August 1991, p. 7.

20 U.S. Special Forces, along with Guatemalan and Israeli trainers, began training a specialized police unit.[90] Then-Security Minister Víctor Emilio Herrera disbanded the unit after a 12 year-old boy was killed during a 1990 anti-drug raid which produced no drugs. Herrera said that no Costa Rican police should be trained by military forces and that "[We] have to act like Costa Ricans, not military men."

However, in September 1991, Costa Rican officials announced that U.S. military personnel, along with Chilean and Taiwanese advisers, will renew training for a specialized anti-narcotics unit within two months. The press reports that drugs is a "recurrent theme" of the new U.S. Ambassador to Costa Rica, Luis Guinot.

* The State Department reports that in April 1991, the Armed Forces of **HONDURAS**, "in collaboration with the U.S. Southern Command, composed a five-year plan which lays out the strategic and supporting operational objectives necessary to establish a functional, efficient military counter-narcotics organization."[91] In March 1991, the Armed Forces Commander of announced the formation of two new anti-drug units within the military.[92] "The Armed Forces is the institution that is most committed to fighting drug trafficking," he said, adding that, "the police corps is also taking very positive steps." He continued, "The Honduran people must trust the Armed Forces because it is taking on its social and economic role."

* In 1991, the government of **EL SALVADOR** set up an Executive Anti-Narcotics Unit drawn from members of the El Salvador Armed Forces and the National Police.[93]

U.S. officials emphasize that the Andean strategy, including the military component, is only in its early stages. In March 1991, Assistant Secretary Levitsky, in response to a question about the overall effectiveness of the strategy, said, "we have a plan. We are following the plan.... Remember the

---

[90] Information in these two paragraphs is from Cyrus Reed, "Boy's Death Sparks Call for Probe," The Tico Times, May 25, 1990; and Edward Orlebar, "Murcielago Base Will Reopen," The Tico Times, September 20, 1991.

[91] 1991 INCSR, p. 152.

[92] These quotes are from the remarks of Armed Forces Commander, Gen. Luis Alonso Discua Elvir, Mar. 27, 1991, San Pedro Sula Tiempo, in Foreign Broadcast Information Service, April 1, 1991, p. 18.

[93] INCSR 1991, p. 142.

President's Andean Strategy was presented as a five-year plan."[94]   One member of Congress gave his impressions from a meeting with Assistant Secretary Bernard Aronson, and Deputy Assistant Secretary of Defense Nancy Dorn: "I think the concluding point they came away with was that...Rome was not built in a day, that this is a five-year strategy, it is going to take awhile, and we need to accustom the American constituency that we are asking to have faith in us to deal with this, to deal in a little bit longer term perspective than a 100-hour war or a three-month event here."[95]

Continued high levels of U.S. military involvement in anti-drugs efforts in the Andes in the coming few years is virtually assured unless the U.S. or Andean governments reverse the momentum of current policy. In April 1990, the Department of Defense submitted a five-year plan for anti-narcotics activities from FY 1992 to FY 1997. 1990 was the first year in which the commanders of the unified commands could begin implementing the counter-narcotics plans called for by Secretary Cheney in September 1989.   In addition, FY 1991 will be the first year in which the Defense Department has a centralized budget for anti-narcotics activities.

SouthCom's three-phase, multi-year plan indicates that the counter-drug mission will remain a priority for some time. Col. Carson and Lt. Col. Tim McMahon, of SouthCom's policy and plans division, told WOLA that SouthCom is anticipating heavy involvement in the drug war for the next five to seven years, even if attention fades in the United States.[96]   Security assistance to Andean countries is part of the Andean Initiative, scheduled to last through FY 1994. Although training of many Andean police has taken place, the U.S. military is only beginning to train and advise the Peruvian armed forces. The military is approaching its counter-narcotics work as it does other missions -- organizing carefully and comprehensively. 1990 was only the first full year of a multi-year effort.

---

[94] Assistant Secretary of State for INM, Melvyn Levitsky, in hearings before the House Foreign Affairs Committee, "Review of the 1991 INCSR," March 5, 7, 12, 13, 1991, p. 46.

[95] Representative Porter Goss (R-Fl), Ibid., p. 52.

[96] Personal interviews, early 1991, Quarry Heights, Panama.

CHAPTER 5

WILL THE ANDEAN STRATEGY WORK?

Chapter Summary

The administration maintains that the Andean strategy is showing progress, but the results to date indicate that the policy is failing. While cocaine use seems to be declining in the U.S., that is not due to any success in cutting supply. Indeed, despite intensified U.S. efforts, the DEA reports that world cocaine production worldwide <u>increased</u> by 28% in 1990.

Furthermore, the logic of the Andean strategy itself reveals the futility of source-country efforts. Rampant corruption, higher governmental priorities in the Andes, and military cooperation with drug traffickers all call into question the strategy's reliance on Andean forces to fight the drug war. Most importantly, even if the strategy's goals of reducing Andean production and disrupting cocaine trafficking could be met, there is no logical link to reduced consumption on U.S. streets because of the ability of producers to move elsewhere and because of the small portion of the price represented by source-country input into the final retail price.

I. THE RESULTS TO DATE

The Bush administration has claimed that its overall federal anti-drug strategy has been successful and that the program is meeting all of its goals. While the administration's statistics are disputed by some experts, cocaine use among occasional users appears to have declined since 1989.[1]

On the international side, the administration is less bullish but maintains that the policy is making progress. The 1991 International Narcotics Control Strategy Report, put out by the State Department, points to the following as the principal achievements of its Andean strategy: (1) Andean coca cultivation levelled off in 1990, and declined in Bolivia and Colombia, (2) drug trafficking in the Andes has been disrupted, raising the cost of doing business, and (3) seizures, arrests, and confiscation of assets have increased in the Andes. Concrete indicators of progress include the reduction of the Medellín cartel's quota of world cocaine distribution from some 75% to possibly as low as 40% and the reduction for the first time in Bolivia's net cocaine production.[2] In addition, increased cooperation by Andean governments and

---

[1] ONDCP, National Drug Control Strategy, 1991.

[2] "Cali Earns a New Reputation: World's No. 1 Cocaine Seller," The New York Times, May 15, 1991.

more antinarcotics activities are cited throughout the report as evidence of progress.

In fact, the administration is falling far short of meeting its principal goal of reducing cocaine availability by 15% by the fall of 1991. The administration states that cocaine production levels increased during the first two years of the Andean strategy.[3] DEA officials report that cocaine production in South America increased from 695 metric tons in 1989 to about 900 metric tons in 1990 -- a **28%** increase.[4] They estimate that in 1991 cocaine production will increase **another 10%**, to 1,000 metric tons. Even production of the coca leaf, as distinct from cocaine, is continuing to increase -- by 4% in the Andes in 1990, according to recently revised State Department statistics.[5]

Although Colombian antinarcotics efforts have disrupted the Medellín cartel's network, those efforts have not had any significant impact on the supply of cocaine into the United States. In fact, U.S. officials have reported that the Colombian government does not foresee having the resources to reduce the supply of cocaine leaving their country.[6] Colombia's vigorous law enforcement efforts -- especially by its police -- certainly complement the Gaviria administration's plea-bargaining strategy toward traffickers and contributed to its success in netting Pablo Escobar and other Medellín leaders. But it is not clear that U.S. assistance played any role in these efforts. Nor is it clear that this step will have any significant impact on quantities of Colombian cocaine reaching the United States. As noted earlier, the three Ochoa brothers, the highest-ranking Medellín leaders after Escobar, reportedly continue to conduct business from their Medellín cells. Moreover, other traffickers -- notably the Cali cartel, which has expanded its operations in Europe to become the world's number 1 cocaine-trafficking organization -- continue to operate relatively unscathed.[7]

Although arrests, seizures, and confiscation of assets in the Andes have increased, they appear to have little relation to drug supply. In the United States, for example, the numbers of arrests for drug possession rose by 107%

---

[3] See testimony of Assistant Administrator David Westrate, DEA, "Operation Snowcap: Past, Present, and Future," before the House Foreign Affairs Committee, May 23, 1990, p. 27; also testimony of Assistant Secretary of State Melvyn Levitsky, "Review of 1991 INCSR...", p. 41.

[4] Christopher Marquis, "Results Meager Year after U.S.-Andean Drug Pact," The Miami Herald, March 13, 1991. Also Douglas Farah, The Washington Post, February 24, 1991.

[5] INCSR 1991.

[6] Michael Skol, Assistant Secretary of State for South America, in "Review of the 1990 International Narcotics Control Strategy Report," hearings before the House Committee on Foreign Affairs, March 1990, p. 150.

[7] "Cali Earns a New Reputation: World's No. 1 Cocaine Seller," op cit.

and for drug sales by 180% between 1980 and 1988.[8] However, DEA figures show that during that time cocaine supply in the U.S. also rose steadily by about 10% per year. Moreover, in the Andes, a large number of arrested suspects have been released because of weak and corrupt judicial systems. In the fall of 1989, Colombia initiated a policy of massive confiscation of the property of suspected drug traffickers. Yet in March 1991, The Washington Post reported that Colombian judicial officials said that their confiscation policy had failed.[9] Because of legal difficulties, the majority of properties have been returned to the suspects, including 230 farms, 192 houses, and 92 airplanes.

Despite the administration's claims of progress, its optimism is not borne out by the record. As one SouthCom official admitted about the military's counter-drug role:

> There's an increasing sense that this is a "holding action". We're not stopping drug supply because it moves. And we could never get the resources to shut down the whole hemisphere. The evidence is that we haven't affected price or supply. Is this the way we want to spend U.S. dollars? I think not.[10]

Measuring Success

For the past decade, U.S. administrations have consistently maintained that their anti-cocaine efforts were making headway, despite the fact that cocaine production has climbed steadily during that time. Congress has questioned the basis for the Executive's persistent optimism, as this example illustrates:

> MR. SMITH: We have not been able to institutionalize [international narcotics control programs]... And that is what is frustrating about sitting here and watching each year the non-institutionalization of the same things...
> The reality is how many years can you go with excuses. Sure, you can always point to some successes, Mr. Levitsky. It is not hard to find some. In some countries, we have had more than in others. But the reality is the law is there specifically to avoid money being thrown down a nonproductive hole. And when you

---

[8] Statistics from The Sentencing Project, "The 'War on Drugs': What Kind of War? Whose Drug Use?", February 25, 1991, p. 1.

[9] Douglas Farah, The Washington Post, Spring 1991 (date unknown).

[10] WOLA Interview with SouthCom official, early 1991.

read the statistical data from year to year, what you find is that it has been nonproductive.[11]

The administration has attempted to justify its hopeful outlook with measures selected to illustrate progress. When examining the progress that has been made, the main U.S. agencies involved in international drug policy cite indicators of supply-side progress without demonstrating how they are linked to success at home. Both the DEA and the State Department carefully publish a variety of indicators of progress, including production and price figures. However, when assessing their overall performance on the international side, they stress statistics on arrests, seizures, hectares eradicated, and labs destroyed. The State Department particularly focuses on the level of cooperation elicited from host governments, as indicated by bilateral accords and mutual agreement on certain activities:

> [CONGRESSMAN] SMITH: Every year we certify [that governments receiving U.S. aid are cooperating with U.S. anti-drug efforts]. Every year we have the certification flying in the face of most of the statistical data, and the answer is that certification is done on the basis of looking at the country's capability to cooperate.
> [ASSISTANT SECRETARY] LEVITSKY: It is.[12]

But a country's "capability to cooperate" has very little to do with the administration's ultimate objective of reducing supply. As shown above, arrests and seizures do not necessarily correlate with reduced supply, and net production figures point to the lack of progress.

An analysis of the Andean strategy's goals shows a vast, unbridged gulf between the problem of cocaine consumption and the putative solution of source-country efforts. The strategy's first three goals focus on "disrupting" drug trafficking (see Chapter 1), and administration officials acknowledge that they have no hope of eliminating cocaine supply. Yet even if trafficking is successfully disrupted for some time in some places, it has no clear impact on overall supply or demand. While disruption may drive up the cost of trafficking, it has not been able (and probably cannot) drive it up sufficiently to make a difference. Furthermore, disruption drives up the cost of repressive efforts by spreading and decentralizing the industry.

---

[11] "Review of the 1990 INCSR," Task Force on International Narcotics Control, House Foreign Affairs Committee, March 1990, p. 163.

[12] Hearings, "Review of the 1990 INCSR...," op cit., p. 162.

Since being pressed into the drug war, the U.S. military has adopted indicators of success that measure its own activities --but do not relate them to the overall goal of reducing cocaine consumption. The Pentagon, whose drug policy coordinator stated publicly in 1988 that DOD feared being a scapegoat for a failed policy, has adopted criteria for evaluating its own performance that are based on the activities carried out rather than their ultimate impact on the strategy's overall objective. DOD spokesman Pete Williams stated in 1990 that Secretary Cheney had decided that successful performance for the military would be measured by how well DOD is "responding to the requests of the law enforcement agencies." In other words, DOD will not look at indicators of successful reduction of supply or demand, but instead will focus on how much equipment has been delivered, how many requests for assistance have been met, etc. The current DOD Drug Policy Coordinator underscored this approach in 1990:

> "...any objective criteria about the number of arrests that are being made or how the cocaine is being confiscated, when we're there to support Customs and border patrol and so forth, I don't think is an accurate measure for the Department of Defense."[13]

The Department has been true to its word. In March 1991, in testimony on DOD's programs in Latin America, then-Assistant Secretary of Defense Henry Rowen listed a page of successful assistance provided to law enforcement agencies -- but only one concrete result -- as evidence of "notable achievements" in the first year of the Andean strategy. That concrete result was the "shift in illegal drug trade to other countries" -- a result which helped to spread the negative effects of cocaine production and trafficking in the hemisphere but has not reduced cocaine production.[14]

II. THE STRATEGY'S CONCEPTUAL FLAWS

Officials confront evidence of lack of progress in the Andean drug war with assertions that with more time (the Andean strategy is only entering its third year), more adjustments and more resources, the problems will be overcome. However, experts and congressional investigations have presented overwhelming evidence that the Andean strategy will not be effective, even with increased investments of resources and time.

---

[13] Assistant Secretary of Defense Stephen Duncan, Drug Coordinator, in official transcript of Press Conference, March 9, 1990, p. 7.

[14] Assistant Secretary of Defense for International Security Affairs Henry Rowen, before the House Appropriations Subcommittee on Foreign Operations, March 13, 1991, pp. 7-8.

The Andean strategy is based on three assumptions, each one of which is highly questionable: (1) that the U.S. government can instill the institutional will to fight the drug war at the level of both Andean governments and Andean militaries; (2) that supply reduction measures will have an effect on price, and therefore demand, for cocaine in the United States; and (3) that supply reduction measures can effectively overcome the "balloon effect."

A. Andean Political Will

Objective #1 of the Andean Strategy is to "strengthen the political commitment and institutional capability of the Governments of Colombia, Peru, and Bolivia" to enable them to disrupt and dismantle cocaine trafficking organizations. However, political will is lacking in the Andes, especially among the armed forces, and the U.S. is unlikely to be able to create that will. Andean militaries are unreliable partners in the drug war. Even if the U.S. can successfully use carrots and sticks to get the Andean governments to agree to bilateral accords signifying governmental cooperation, there is little guarantee that Andean military forces will use U.S. assistance and training in the ways envisioned by the United States. Corruption is rampant among state forces, and in Colombia and Peru, U.S. anti-drug aid used for counterinsurgency is likely to have few -- or negative -- effects in curbing drug production and trafficking.

Governmental Priorities

While drug policy dominates U.S. foreign policy toward the Andes, the governments of the region see their priorities differently. The two principal problems they face are economic crisis and political unrest, including armed insurgencies in Peru and Colombia. By comparison, fighting drug trafficking is a low priority for Andean governments, and agreeing to "cooperate" in the U.S. drug war is a way of garnering resources for other problems.

Currently Peru faces the most serious economic crisis and political unrest on the continent, but has been the most successful of the three governments at getting the U.S. administration to endorse using anti-drug monies to address those priorities. President Fujimori's anti-inflationary "fujishock" has deepened an ongoing recession, and one official characterized the continuing crisis by saying, "Desperation is our only hope." The Shining Path guerrillas, the most brutal insurgent movement on the continent, have increased in strength over the past two years. Disrupting coca production and trafficking could drive peasants into the hands of insurgents -- and at the same time take away desperately-needed foreign exchange now propping up the economy.[15] The Fujimori government believes that a socio-economic approach to the drug situation can help both the economy and its counterinsurgency efforts. It sees the U.S. military approach as aggravating these other problems.

At the same time, the Fujimori administration recognizes the need to reach an anti-drug accord with the United States in order not to remain cut off from the international financial community. The accord clearly states that U.S. security assistance can be used for counterinsurgency purposes in the Huallaga Valley, as the Peruvian military has insisted. Yet it is not clear what degree of cooperation may be expected if the drug war begins to conflict significantly with the government's higher priorities. Given the tensions between antinarcotics and counterinsurgency -- and given the importance of coca revenues to the economy -- such a scenario is conceivable.

In Bolivia, the government is also engaged in a difficult balancing act. On one side, it understands the need for U.S. good will to enjoy access to the international and U.S. financial community. On the other, it has interests in retaining foreign exchange generated by the cocaine industry and in minimizing public criticism and protest over highly unpopular antinarcotics programs. The government has faced formidable opposition to U.S.-backed antinarcotics programs -- opposition that must be taken into account at election time. Cocaine revenue is essential to the success of the government's economic program. According to Bolivia's former Minister of Finance, Flavio Machicado, "If narcotics were to disappear overnight, we would have rampant unemployment. There would be open protest and violence." By conservative estimates, the coca/cocaine industry employs approximately 75,000 families and thousands more benefit from other jobs generated by it.[16] While the Paz Zamora government has haltingly moved ahead with the antinarcotics program laid out in the bilateral accord with the United States, it remains a reluctant player in the drug war.

Colombia's own version of the "war on drugs" has been very different from the U.S. model. Colombia's war has focused on ending terrorist acts carried out by drug traffickers (the "narcoterrorism" of kidnappings, assassination of hundreds of police officers and public office-holders, and random bombing of civilians) rather than ending drug-trafficking per se (i.e., trafficking cocaine for profit). Colombia's latest campaign against narcoterrorism was sparked by the assassination, almost certainly by the

---

[15] See, e.g., "U.S. Government Anti-Narcotics Activities in the Andean Region of South America," Report by the Permanent Subcommittee on Investigations of the Senate Committee on Governmental Affairs, February 6, 1990, which points out these factors soon after the Andean strategy was announced.

[16] Peter Andreas, "Coca Denial," NACLA Report on the Americas, op cit.

Medellín cartel, of presidential candidate Luis Carlos Galán, in August 1989. Since that cartel has been responsible for almost all of Colombia's narcoterrorism, it has been the target of the government's war on drugs. The Cali cartel has been relatively untouched by governmental antinarcotics activities, and its leaders continue to travel freely in that city, sometimes with police escorts. As one law enforcement official said, "They never challenged the political structure, they just bought it."

Recent events may strain Colombia's cooperation with U.S. anti-drug efforts. In late 1990, President Gaviria offered not to extradite and to reduce sentences for any drug traffickers who turned themselves in and confessed to one drug-related crime. The offer netted the Medellín cartel's top leaders, including Pablo Escobar. The policy of extraditing drug traffickers to the U.S., feared by the traffickers, was long controversial in Colombia, and in June 1991 the Constituent Assembly voted to ban extradition. These measures are clearly aimed at ending narcoterrorism, but experts doubt that they will substantially diminish drug-trafficking. The DEA reports that the Cali cartel has increased its sales in Europe in the past two years, and that it now controls 70% of the cocaine entering the United States.[17] Top cartel leaders live openly in Cali, and one European diplomat in Bogotá predicted after Escobar's surrender that "the Government is not going to touch the [Cali cartel] leaders."[18] In addition, top Colombian law enforcement officials have claimed that the Ochoa brothers continue to run drug trafficking operations from their cell.[19] One journalist summed up a common sentiment in Colombia:

> ...let there be no misunderstanding. What [Gaviria's government is] trying to resolve is narco-terrorism. Nobody in Colombia talks seriously about ending narco-trafficking. Why should they?[20]

While there are no specific signs that U.S.-Colombian military cooperation will decline, anti-drug cooperation between the two countries in the future is likely to depend largely on the criminal proceedings against Pablo Escobar and on Colombian antinarcotics efforts against other cartels such as that of Cali.

---

[17] "New Kings of Coke," Time, July 1, 1991.

[18] James Brooke, "Cali, The 'Quiet' Drug Cartel, Profits by Accommodation," The New York Times, July 14, 1991.

[19] Douglas Farah, "Colombia Said to Face Trafficking from Jail," The Washington Post, May 29, 1991.

[20] Cecilia Rodríguez, "Jailing a Feared Narco-Terrorist Won't End Narco-Trafficking," The Los Angeles Times, June 9, 1991.

Corruption

Corruption is rampant in Andean security forces, especially the police, even after years of antinarcotics assistance there. A few particularly vivid examples:

BOLIVIA:

* In 1988 Bolivian Navy officers held two DEA agents incommunicado at gunpoint and helped several traffickers escape arrest by antinarcotics police.

* In March 1991, the Minister of the Interior and the head of Bolivia's anti-drug police resigned amid charges that they were involved in drug trafficking. President Paz Zamora had appointed the latter as head of the antinarcotics police despite his Cabinet post in the García Meza regime that took power in the 1980 "cocaine coup."

* In April 1991, the Bolivian government announced that much of the leadership of the UMOPAR antinarcotics police would be dismissed because of corruption. The UMOPAR has been the principal recipient of U.S. Special Forces training in the Andes, and the need for such wholesale housecleaning indicates the weakness of claims that years of U.S. training can remedy this fundamental problem.

PERU:

* In two separate incidents during the second week of March 1990, Peruvian police units travelling in U.S.-owned helicopters were fired upon by military personnel.

* SouthCom's Special Forces commander stated that there is "unbelievable corruption" among Peruvian state forces, and that "We know as a fact that the Army gets payments for letting traffickers use airstrips."

* In early 1991, the military cooperated with drug traffickers in foiling a police raid against traffickers.

COLOMBIA:

* As of late 1989, the office of Colombia's Attorney General was investigating 4,200 cases of corruption by police and some 1,700 involving the armed forces.

Bolivian and Peruvian authorities have openly stated their concerns that involving the military in antinarcotics will extend corruption to that institution rather than make for more effective antinarcotics efforts. The U.S. government may contribute to, rather than curb, drug trafficking by giving assistance to forces that are endemically penetrated by corruption.

Competing Military Priorities

Both the armed forces and the police of the Andean countries have been very much opposed to an expanded military role in antinarotics activities. The militaries of Colombia, Peru, and Bolivia welcome U.S. security assistance and have adapted their missions sufficiently to obtain such aid. However, it is unclear that these Andean militaries will use U.S. antinarotics assistance in the ways intended by Congress. Furthermore, a wide array of Andean civilian and police officials, scholars, and other experts have cast doubt on whether Andean militaries can make a positive difference in the drug war.

In <u>Colombia</u>, the army stated that $38.5 of $40.3 million in U.S. counternarcotics military aid for FY 1990 would be destined for an unrelated counterinsurgency operation. Although in the past year the military has participated in more counternarcotics operations, Colombian government officials and experts maintain that its role remains marginal to that of the police, and some claim that military involvement is counterproductive.

> The Colombian military hasn't wanted to get involved in antinarotics. They've been pressed by the Colombian government as well as by the United States. To the military this war is unwinnable, not crucial to national defense, creates problems with morale and corruption, hurts relations with campesinos and diverts important military resources. An increased military participation in the drug war has the effect of creating more guerrillas.[21]

Another Colombian expert echoed these sentiments, "Increased military assistance from the United States has had no positive impact on the production of cocaine. If the military are turning up more cocaine it's only because there's more out there... Increasing repression... will never stop the drugs from coming into the United States."[22]

Some Colombian officials are surprisingly frank about the military's irrelevance to antinarotics efforts in Colombia. One police Captain said:

> "It's a lie that we need the army to get into certain areas. The army isn't losing men. They're not fighting. We haven't conducted a single operation with the support of the army. We don't need the military. We've done it all alone.

---

[21] Jochnick interviews.

[22] Jochnick interview with Professor, National University.

Where the army is strong, for instance in La Uribe, there are no laboratories. We have attacked the labs where the guerrillas are strong. We have the ability.

The military is fighting the guerrillas. They armed the self-defense groups and then the traffickers started supporting these groups. For instance in the Magdalena Medio, during the Primavera Operation we found lots of labs. The military did not help us with this operation nor in any of our other operations. The only help the military has provided the anti-narcotics police is letting them stay in military bases.

Q: IS THE ARMY ATTACKING THE PARAMILITARY GROUPS?
No. They're not fighting against the paramilitary groups. They're fighting the guerrillas.

Q: IS THE MILITARY ACTUALLY HINDERING YOU WITH ITS LINKS TO THE PARAMILITARY GROUPS?
[They] could be."[23]

The following are excerpts from an interview with Dr. Rafael Pardo, then-National Security Adviser to President Gaviria:
"Q: WHAT'S THE ROLE OF THE MILITARY IN COUNTERNARCOTICS?
The military gives some support when necessary.
Q: IS IT FREQUENTLY NECESSARY?
When there are big operations.
Q: ARE THERE FREQUENTLY BIG OPERATIONS?
Not so many. Increasingly the labs are being broken down into smaller labs which the police are capable of handling themselves without need for military support. The police can handle almost all the problems by themselves."[24]

His comments were echoed by Dr. Germán Cano, Colombia's Interpol chief:
"Q: WHAT ROLE DOES THE MILITARY PLAY IN COUNTERNARCOTICS?
By law the armed forces are the chief anti-narcotics agency. In terms of figures, the police have done most of the work. The army is busy with the guerrillas. They can't concentrate exclusively on anti-narcotics.
Q: WHAT DOES COLOMBIA NEED FOR THE DRUG WAR?

---

[23] Captain Segura, Anti-narcotics Police (DAN), Jochnick interview, Summer 1991, op cit.

[24] Jochnick interview with Dr. Pardo. Pardo was appointed Minister of Defense in 1991.

We need intelligence equipment more than anything else. Operations fail for lack of intelligence or infiltration, never for lack of arms or helicopters."[25]

In <u>Bolivia</u>, President Paz Zamora stated that FY 1990 U.S. military assistance to the army would be used for environmental activities. At the same time that his troops were preparing to fly to Bolivia to begin training the Bolivian army, SouthCom's top Special Forces commander said that for counternarcotics efforts to work in Bolivia, the armed forces "must have the intent to become successful, and I don't think they do."[26]

And in <u>Peru</u>, where the administration advocates using antinarcotics assistance for counterinsurgency efforts against the Shining Path, the military has been openly hostile to the anti-drug mission, impeding police operations in areas under their control. As then-commander of the Upper Huallaga Valley told WOLA,

"If we attack drug trafficking, we will convert the local population into our enemy... Instead of one enemy, the Shining Path, we will have three: the Shining Path, the local population who will then support the Shining Path, and the drug traffickers who will then provide resources to the Shining path."[27]

B. The Minimal Impact of Source-Country Efforts on Demand

In testimony before Congress in early 1991, RAND Corporation economist Peter Reuter stated that, "Source country programs, whether they be crop eradication, crop substitution or refinery destruction, hold negligible prospect for reducing American cocaine consumption in the long-run." Reuter's analysis shows that:

* Coca leaf farmers receive less than 1% of the final retail price of cocaine,
* Earnings for cocaine exporters and smugglers comprise less than 15% of the final price.

---

[25] Jochnick interview, <u>op cit.</u>, with Dr. Cano.

[26] WOLA Interview with Col. Robert Jacobelly, Commander, Special Operations Command South (SOCSOUTH), Panama, early 1991.

[27] WOLA Interview with General Brito, Commander, San Martín department, Peru, October 1990.

Because over 85% of cocaine profits are made outside the source countries, source-country efforts will not drive up the retail price in the U.S. enough to significantly reduce cocaine consumption. According to this analysis, even if interdiction efforts were able to stop the extremely unlikely figure of 50% of cocaine shipments from Colombia, the retail price of cocaine in the United States would rise by less than 3%. No one has presented data to refute Reuter's analysis.

C. The "Balloon Effect"

Most importantly, even if current Andean suppression efforts are successful, DEA officials acknowledge that production is likely to simply spread to other countries. This dispersion, which some call the "balloon effect" (i.e., squeezing in one place produces expansion into other places), has occurred in previous antinarcotics campaigns in Turkey and Mexico, and is already occurring in the current drug war. In the late 1980s, U.S. interdiction efforts led traffickers to shift from air drops in Southern Florida to air drops over the Caribbean Sea for pick-up by boat. Subsequent efforts led traffickers to shift to air drops into Northern Mexico, which are taken by land into the U.S.

In the Andes themselves, the balloon effect has occurred on a scale that has surprised U.S. anti-drug officials. One SouthCom official said, "[Cocaine production and trafficking] has decentralized much more than we ever thought it would."[28] Colombian traffickers have shifted to more numerous, smaller labs in order to impede counternarcotics efforts and are relying more on processing labs in Bolivia and Peru. The latter two countries are now producing over 100 metric tons of cocaine per year --about 10% each of the world total.[29] In addition, Uruguay and Argentina have become important money laundering centers, and the latter has become a key transshipment point for Europe. Moreover, cocaine processing and transshipment has increased significantly in Brazil, Venezuela, and Ecuador in recent months.

The Bush administration and others have responded to the problems posed by the balloon effect and other impediments by escalating the drug war. In the case of Peru, the administration continues to explore the possibility of using a herbicide to eradicate the coca crop. In 1991, the administration reported that follow-up testing had been conducted in 1990 on the environmental effects of the herbicide Tebuthiuron ("Spike"). The State Department said that analysis "revealed no long-term detrimental effects" from

---

[28] Personal interview, mid-1991.

[29] Information in this paragraph is from Gary Marx, "Drug Trade Spreads in South America," The Chicago Tribune, August 18, 1991.

the use of Spike.[30]   Environmental groups such as Greenpeace, which challenged the administration's initial Environmental Assessment as "patently false," continue to express concern over the effects of herbicides on human and plant life.[31]   The coca growers of the region oppose use of such a herbicide because its potential environmental devastation could deprive them of a livelihood before they even had any viable alternative. As of 1991, the Peruvian government had put consideration of herbicides on hold, and the Bush administration has claimed that "Full-scale herbicidal eradication does not appear politically feasible at this time."[32]   But due to the balloon effect, even the use of herbicides may not prevent the spread of cocaine production to other countries.

U.S. agencies involved in antinarcotics are already seeing how their institutional programs (and budgets) can be expanded to counter the balloon effect.   The State Department is extending its efforts with countries neighboring the Andean Initiative countries.[33]   The DEA has begun an operation equivalent to Operation Snowcap in Guatemala, and is anticipating parallel programs to combat increased heroin trafficking.[34]   DEA Assistant Administrator David Westrate's testimony suggests the extraordinary resources that would have to be marshalled to apply a Snowcap-style operation to the heroin trade:

> My big worry... for future years, and I am talking three to five, is the heroin situation. Heroin is going to be ten times more difficult to deal with than this cocaine situation, because cocaine basically comes from two fairly isolated areas. You are dealing with one language. When you talk about heroin, you are probably dealing with a dozen different languages. You are dealing with three wide-scattered source areas... So I think that is really the big challenge that we are up against internationally in five years."[35]

And the military is already trying to expand its antinarcotics programs in South America, planning elaborate operations based on the riverine systems

---

[30] INCSR, March 1991, p. 116.

[31] See "Cocaine Production, Eradication, and the Environment: Policy, Impact, and Options," seminar held by the Congressional Research Service, August 1990, Senate Print 101-110, esp. Greenpeace, "Briefing Paper, State Department's Coca Eradication Spray Program in Peru." Phone interview with Sandra Marquardt, Greenpeace, August 1991.

[32] INCSR op cit.

[33] "Review of the 1990 INCSR," Hearings before the House Committee on Foreign Affairs, March 1990, p. 131.

[34] Interview with Charles Gutensohn, op cit.

[35] David Westrate, DEA Asst. Administrator for Operations, hearings before House Foreign Affairs Committee, "Review of the 1990 INCSR, March 1990, p. 98.

primarily of the Amazon -- despite the fact that there are about 75,000 boats estimated to be on the Amazon at any one time.

It is inconceivable that the U.S. could finance the aid and U.S. personnel, and also secure the continent-wide host country cooperation, necessary to eliminate coca production militarily throughout Latin America. Colombia, Bolivia, and Peru themselves cover an area equal to the United States east of the Mississippi. Brazil, which U.S. officials are especially worried about because of its vast size, has already turned down offers of U.S. military trainers.[36]

---

[36] On Brazil's response, author interview with SouthCom official.

CHAPTER 6

NEGATIVE CONSEQUENCES:
THE ANDEAN STRATEGY, HUMAN RIGHTS, AND DEMOCRATIZATION

Chapter Summary

Current U.S. antinarcotics policy in the Andes is likely to be not only ineffective against drug trafficking but counterproductive for human rights, political violence, and democracy. Although the Bush administration has taken some positive steps to mitigate negative consequences, there is strong evidence that the current strategy may aggravate human rights violations and undermine democratization processes in the region. The human rights records of Colombian and Peruvian government forces are among the very worst in the hemisphere. Andean human rights organizations believe that U.S. drug-related security assistance could well fuel those human rights abuses. As in the case of Central America in the 1980s, the U.S. government is allying itself with abusive militaries before those forces observe even minimal standards of human rights and international humanitarian law.

Concern is widespread in Bolivia and Peru that involving the armed forces, especially the army, in the drug war will strengthen the hands of the military at the expense of civilian institutions. There, as in most of Latin America, increased attention is being given to strengthening civilian institutions such as the judiciary, political parties and executive agencies. However, the Andean strategy views as essential an expanded role for the military in a new internal security matter. Within governments and societies in the Andes there is considerable concern that involving the armed forces in a new internal security role will undermine civilian control of the military, and thus democracy itself.

Furthermore, the Andean strategy may aggravate political violence in the region. Andean experts believe that the strategy's military component plays into the hands of guerrilla groups, which use "U.S. intervention" to gain the support of the local populations affected by militarized antinarcotics programs. In Peru, opposition to U.S. antinarcotics policy has reportedly brought peasants into the ranks of the Shining Path guerrillas. In both Peru and Bolivia, violent confrontations have taken place between antinarcotics forces and local civilian populations. In Bolivia, coca growers have threatened to defend their livelihood with their lives, and a few coca growers federations have pledged to form self-defense groups if faced with Bolivian army operations.

108

I. HUMAN RIGHTS AND THE WAR ON DRUGS

Commendably, U.S. legislation and international antinarcotics accords include provisions relating to the protection of human rights. The Declaration of Cartagena requires that "the parties act within the framework for human rights" and states that "nothing would do more to undermine the war on drugs than disregard for human rights." The memorandum of understanding between Peru and the United States attaches "great importance" to implementing anti-drug programs in accord with international standards of human rights, explicitly mentioning prohibitions on extrajudicial executions, disappearances, torture, and other abuses. Section 502(B) of the Foreign Assistance Act states that a government may not receive security assistance if it "engages in a consistent pattern of gross violations of internationally recognized human rights." Strengthening human rights is listed as one of the objectives of drug-related military aid in the International Narcotics Control Act of 1990, and that act initiated a requirement that the President issue a "determination" that recipients of security assistance have "made significant progress in protecting internationally recognized human rights."[1]

Although the Andean strategy continues to enjoy broad bipartisan support in Congress, some members of Congress have expressed concern over the implications of the Andean strategy for human rights. Congressman Ted Weiss asserted in 1990 that "the Bush Administration's determination to send millions of dollars in military aid to the Andean region, for example, is having a profoundly negative impact on our efforts to promote human rights...".[2] In hearings in 1991, Representative Robert Torricelli, Chairman of the Western Hemisphere Subcommittee in the House, expressed his concerns about U.S. military aid supporting counterinsurgency campaigns "characterized by widespread violation of human rights."[3] And a House Government Operations Committee Report issued in November 1990, stated that "The Committee is deeply concerned that U.S. military aid may exacerbate human rights abuses in Colombia..."[4]

The administration says that human rights are a serious concern in carrying out the Andean strategy. Assistant Secretary Levitsky said in 1991, "Let me say my office is certainly concerned about human rights and personally I am because I used to be a Deputy Assistant Secretary for Human

---

[1] That requirement, in Section 4(a), explicitly listed a variety of violations such as torture, disappearances, incommunicado detention, and stated that appropriate international organizations (e.g., the Red Cross) should have unimpeded access to detention centers.

[2] Statement in opposition to the Feighan Anti-Narcotics Amendment, May 22, 1990.

[3] "Review of the 1991 INCSR..." op cit., March 7, 1991, p. 69.

[4] "U.S. Anti-Narcotics Activities in the Andean Region," op cit., p. 94.

Rights."[5] The administration reports that "We cannot gloss over past abuses in some countries. The U.S. opposes these abuses as a matter of national policy and always will." SouthCom officials report that the CINC has eight essential joint mission tasks, and that "human rights is one of them."[6]

In applying these human rights concerns to the Andes, the Bush administration justifies security assistance to governments there on several grounds. First, the administration claims (as in its 1991 determinations) that the governments of Colombia, Peru and Bolivia do not engage in a "consistent" pattern of gross violations. Second, the administration claims (as in its 1991 determinations) that the governments of Peru, Colombia, Bolivia and Ecuador made "significant progress" in protecting human rights during 1990. Third, the administration points out that drug traffickers and leftist insurgents engage in human rights abuses: "we should not succumb to the notion that organizations like the Sendero Luminoso of Peru or the FARC in Colombia are champions of human rights."[7]

Fourth, the administration claims that the Andean strategy includes human rights training on a number of levels. The administration reports that "Special Forces MTTs are required to teach respect for human rights... in both formal classroom lectures/discussions and in practical hands-on instruction," and in 1991 an inter-agency task force began implementing mandatory human rights training for all relevant U.S. personnel that will serve in countries where human rights violations occur.[8] Finally and perhaps most importantly, the administration claims that "disengagement" from Andean militaries would only worsen their human rights records:

"[The human rights situation] is a very serious thing, and we take it very seriously. On the other hand, we do not think that disengaging from this and isolating the military is going to make it any better... That is, if we are involved with them, they will respect human rights more, rather than less, and we will have ways of tracking that..."[9]

---

[5] "Review of 1991 INCSR...", op cit., p. 96.

[6] Personal interview, Gen. John Ellerson, J-3, Quarry Heights, Panama, early 1991.

[7] Joint report by Departments of Defense and State, transmitted in February 1991, op cit.

[8] Quote from the joint report issued by the Departments of Defense and State, op cit. Training program described in inter-agency memoranda, 1991.

[9] Assistant Secretary Levitsky, in hearings, "Review of the 1990 INCSR...," March 1990, pp. 115-116.

Dangers for Human Rights

Despite its attention to human rights concerns, the administration has not demonstrated sufficient recognition of the complexities in -- and government responsibilities for -- the human rights situation in each of the Andean countries.

First, the administration has not consistently emphasized human rights in presenting and justifying its antinarcotics programs. Immediately after stating his "personal" interest in human rights, Assistant Secretary Levitsky continued, "But our focus is really on the drug issue."[10] Indeed, it is surprising that -- when asked a question citing the language in Section 502(b), the cornerstone provision concerning human rights in all U.S. foreign assistance programs -- this top U.S. official for anti-drug programs in the Andes, a former Deputy Assistant Secretary for Human Rights, would reply, "I am sorry that on the human rights side, I don't know specifically what the law states".[11] Despite SouthCom officials' claims, the promotion of human rights is absent from the entire Southern Theater Strategy except for one mention among general U.S. foreign policy goals in the region.[12] And in the nine-page military annex agreement with Bolivia, human rights are mentioned not once (see Appendix B).

Second, the administration understates the consistency of governmental human rights violations in both Colombia and Peru. Despite Colombia's history of formal democracy, the gross violations of human rights by state security forces -- military and police -- are well documented.[13] Section 502(B) of the foreign assistance act lists the following as some of the abuses included in "gross" violations: "torture or cruel, inhuman, or degrading treatment or punishment, prolonged detention without charges and trial, ...disappearance..., and other flagrant denial of the right to life, liberty, or the security of the person." The State Department's Country Report on Human Rights in Colombia states that in 1990, "Members and

---

[10] Ibid., p. 96.

[11] Assistant Secretary of State for INM, Melvyn Levitsky, in hearings before the House Foreign Affairs Committee, "The Andean initiative," June 20, 1990, p. 132.

In hearings before a subcommittee of the House Committee on Banking, Finance and Urban Affairs on August 5, 1982, Levitsky (then-Deputy Assistant Secretary of State for Human Rights and Humanitarian Affairs) was sufficiently familiar with human rights legislation to say that "...Guatemala cannot be considered by any standard of measurement to be a country in which there is a consistent pattern of gross violations of human rights." Quoted in Joy Hackel and Daniel Siegel, eds. In Contempt of Congress, Institute for Policy Studies, Washington DC, 1987, p. 123.

[12] SouthCom, "Southern Theater Strategy," op cit. "Human rights" are not mentioned in SouthCom's theater strategic objectives, its Andean ridge objectives, its counter-narcotics task list, or its counter-insurgency task list.

[13] Non-state actors also commit grave abuses of basic human rights. These include paramilitary squads that collaborate with armed forces personnel in violating human rights, drug traffickers that engage in narcoterrorism, and leftist insurgent groups that violate laws of war.

units of the army and police participated in a disturbing number of human rights violations including extrajudicial executions, torture, and massacres" against leftist politicians, human rights monitors, and labor and peasant leaders.[14] Colombian human rights organizations uniformly claim that, despite initiation of important reforms which could eventually improve the human rights situation, government forces continue to engage in extrajudicial executions, torture, massacres, disappearances, and other human rights violations.[15]

Although Section 502(B) lists abuses that fall within "gross violations," it does not define "consistent pattern."[16] Yet significant evidence substantiates a consistent pattern of abuses by Colombian state forces. The testimony of ex-operatives supports allegations of Colombian military institutional approval at least at the regional level, both tacit and in some cases explicit, of killings, disappearance and torture.[17] The frequency of such abuses also illustrates their consistency. Americas Watch states with regard to government agents' violations of human rights: "These cases are frequent enough that they constitute a pattern."[18] In a recent case of military abuse on April 7, 1991, 17 persons were taken off a public bus by soldiers and, according to the International Human Rights Working Group, subsequently killed by paramilitary group with the support of local soldiers in Los Uvos, a small

---

[14] U.S. State Department, "Country Reports on Human Rights," February 1991, submitted to Congress, Senate Report 102-5, p. 548.

[15] According to the Centro de Investigación y Educación Popular, a respected non-governmental research institute in Colombia, 2,311 Colombian non-combatants were assassinated in 1990 for reasons that were politically motivated or presumed to be politically motivated. Another 217 were "disappeared."
   Recent reforms are various, but human rights groups are skeptical that they will end what are considered to be gross violations of human rights. A new constitution has been drafted; certain paramilitary groups have demobilized; the judicial system has been revamped; four guerrilla groups have laid down their arms; and the government is negotiating with the FARC and the ELN. In addition, the Gaviria administration has announced a National Strategy Against Violence in which the government pledges to end impunity.
   Yet the International Human Rights Working Group, a coalition of eight of Colombia's leading human rights groups, notes that between January and May of this year, 807 Colombians were killed for political or presumably political reasons, 174 were victims of social "clean-up" campaigns (against such persons as the homeless, homosexuals, and prostitutes) and 69 were disappeared. International Human Rights Working Group, "Quinto llamado internacional sobre la situación de derechos humanos en Colombia," primer semestre de 1991, p. 1.

[16] Foreign Assistance Act of 1961 as amended. Although the U.S. government has withheld or cut off aid for human rights performance, it has never formally invoked Section 502(B) to declare that a government engages in a "consistent pattern of gross violations of human rights."

[17] In August 1989, Ricardo Gámez Mazuera, a Colombian national formerly employed as an "extraofficial" civilian intelligence operative (1978-1989) by army and police intelligence units, gave testimony before a notary public, submitted to the Procurator General. The testimony detailed the role of the military units, including particularly that of the Batallón de Inteligencia y Contrainteligencia "Charry Solano" (BINCI), in human rights violations. See Amnesty International, "Colombia: Human Rights Developments, 'Death Squads on the Defensive?'", Appendix, September 1989, London, p. 7. As always, it is difficult to verify such testimony.

[18] Americas Watch, The "Drug War" in Colombia..., op cit., p. 73.

112

hamlet in the municipality of Bolívar (Cauca).[19] The Permanent Tribunal of the Peoples characterized the government's behavior as one of "systematic and permanent violation of the most basic rights."[20]

The pattern of impunity also testifies to the consistency of government human rights violations. The Gaviria administration has taken important steps toward ending military impunity, but a lack of accountability continues to prevail. The State Department states that "certain violators" of human rights have been dismissed from the military and police following investigations, but that "sanctions for human rights abuses seldom extend beyond dismissal from the service" and that "efforts by security forces to end such abuses have been inadequate."[21] In late 1990, Americas Watch claimed that, "Not surprisingly, there have been successful prosecutions of human rights violations in only three cases:

> Attempts by the government and by prosecutor and judges to investigate and punish [human rights violators] have not significantly reduced their occurrence... The military high command, in our view, not only fails to do enough to stop these actions, but on some occasions deliberately shields and protects their agents from serious investigation."[22]

Gross violations by the security forces of <u>Peru</u> are also well documented. These occur principally in the context of the internal war against two principal guerrilla groups, the Sendero Luminoso (Shining Path) guerrillas and the MRTA (the Spanish acronym for the Túpac Amaru Revolutionary Movement). For the fourth year in a row, in 1990 the Commission on Human Rights of the United Nations received more reports from Peru of "disappearance" following detention by security forces than from any other country in the world. The 1990 State Department human rights report notes:

> "widespread credible reports of summary executions, arbitrary detentions, and torture and rape by the military, as well as less frequent reports of such abuses by the police. Rape by members of the security forces is reported to be so frequent that such abuse can be considered common practice, condoned -- or at least ignored by the military leadership."

---

[19] <u>Ibid.</u>, p. 4.

[20] Quoted in International Human Rights Working Group, <u>op cit.</u>, p. 2.

[21] U.S. State Department, <u>Country Reports on Human Rights Practices for 1990</u>, February 1991, p. 549.

[22] Americas Watch, <u>The "Drug War" in Colombia...</u>, <u>op cit</u>.

In July 1991, in its human rights determination required for delivery of antinarcotics security assistance, the Bush administration claimed that Peruvian security forces do not engage in a consistent pattern of gross violations of human rights. Key committee chairmen of both the House and the Senate suspended economic and military assistance to Peru in late July 1991 principally because of questions about the determination. In addition, some members of Congress denounced the determination. Representative Ted Weiss (D-NY) called the determination "shameful and fraudulent," and said that "until real progress is made, not one dime of aid should be released."[23]

There is widespread agreement among national and international human rights groups that the human rights violations of Peruvian security forces constitute a consistent pattern. In a letter protesting the determination, the National Human Rights Coordinating Committee, Peru's main human rights umbrella group, cited three recent massacres, several extrajudicial executions, and a number of disappearances within the past three months as evidence of the consistency of violations by Peruvian security forces.[24] They also pointed to killings by police officers and to a recently leaked document of the Ministry of Defense that called for the elimination of presumed subversives "without leaving traces".[25] The committee concluded,

"All of these facts reveal that human rights violations are not isolated events -- as could happen anywhere in the world -- but are the result of a pattern of conduct consistently used by the security forces, whose Commander in Chief is, constitutionally, the President of the Republic."[26]

Peruvian human rights groups especially rejected the Bush administration's claim in the determination that "Peru's major human rights groups" concur that the government's practices do not constitute a 'consistent' pattern: "That is an outrageous lie," said Pilar Coll, head of the National Human Rights Coordinating Committee.[27] The State Department's 1990 human rights report describes Peru's counterinsurgency campaign as one of "widespread and egregious human rights violations." In March 1991 Congressional hearings

---

[23] Representative Ted Weiss, quoted in Reuters wire report, July 30, 1991. See also the comments of Representative Torricelli in the same, and letter from Senators Kennedy, Cranston and Dodd and Representatives Weiss, Gejdenson, Berman, among others, to President Bush, July 23, 1991.

[24] Coordinadora Nacional de Derechos Humanos, letter to Ambassador Quainton, August 1, 1991, WOLA's translation.

[25] Ibid. One month after the release of the Defense Ministry document its author was dismissed from the armed forces.

[26] Javier Ciurlizza, Coordinadora Nacional de Derechos Humanos, quoted in Sam Dillon, "Rights Advocates in Peru Criticize Report from US.," The Miami Herald, August 22, 1991.

[27] Ibid.

before the House Western Hemisphere Subcommittee, Bernard Aronson, Assistant Secretary of State for Inter-American Affairs, described abuses by the Peruvian security forces as "long-standing and systemic."

Third, the administration's claims of improvement in Peru and Bolivia are contradicted by human rights groups as well as the State Department's own human rights report. In <u>Bolivia</u>, the human rights situation deteriorated in the last months of 1990, although it remains far less grave than that of Colombia and Peru. In its annual report on human rights, the State Department documented well-known cases of torture and cruelty by police and army intelligence units, as well as extrajudicial executions of detainees.[28] These abuses escalated toward the end of the year, and were largely focused on suspected "terrorists" of the recently emerged Néstor Paz Zamora Command (CNPZ) and the Armed Forces of Liberation Zárate Willka.[29]

<u>Peruvian</u> human rights groups disagree with State Department claims that the human rights situation in that country progressed in 1990. Pilar Coll's assessment bears repeating: "The Peruvian security forces systematically violate the most fundamental human rights...the situation has gotten no better over the last year."[30] The State Department itself notes that "For the fourth straight year, political and other extrajudicial killings rose again in 1990."[31] Indeed, administration officials privately admit that the determination contradicts the statistics, but fall back on the argument that disengagement would exact a higher cost than initiating U.S. drug-related military aid.

Fourth, abuses by drug traffickers and insurgents in no way mitigates the U.S.' responsibility to abide by laws governing foreign assistance and to hold recipients accountable for their treatment of their citizens. Drug mafias and guerrillas are indeed responsible for acts of terrorism and abuses of civilians and other non-combatants and should be held accountable. Yet deflecting concerns about the human rights records of recipients of U.S. aid by citing the abuses of traffickers and insurgents implies that governmental abuses may somehow be balanced against violations by non-state actors. Citizens' rights not to be killed, tortured, disappeared, or treated cruelly or inhumanely are absolute guarantees under international law, not to be set aside under any circumstances.

---

[28] U.S. State Department, <u>Country Reports on Human Rights Practices for 1990</u>, pp. 515-518.

[29] <u>Ibid</u>. See also WOLA, <u>Latin America Update</u>, January-April 1991.

[30] Personal interview, July 31, 1991.

[31] U.S. State Department, <u>Country Reports ...</u>, <u>op cit.</u>, pp. 737.

Fifth, there is no evidence that current human rights training for foreign military forces departs significantly from previous programs, nor that it is based on a thorough evaluation of the effectiveness of such training in past U.S. security assistance programs. The U.S. executive branch has for many years argued that military training programs in Latin America include human rights components,[32] as for example with the training provided to Salvadoran and Guatemalan forces in the 1980s.[33] Whether these training programs actually contribute to better human rights observance by trainees has been questioned by human rights monitors; there is no evidence that it does.[34] Human rights training in the Andes appears not to differ at all from that done previously in Latin America. Although the administration claims that a human rights training curriculum is mandatory, when questioned about it SouthCom's Chief of Counternarcotics, Col. Keith Nightingale, responded that "human rights is not a curricular subject."[35] SouthCom reports that trainers address treatment of wounded civilians and combatants, but no written materials on human rights training for foreign forces were produced by U.S. military officials when WOLA requested to see any such materials. More fundamentally, there is no convincing evidence that such materials would make a difference in how the forces trained actually behave.

The administration is taking steps toward providing human rights training for U.S. personnel assigned to posts in U.S. embassies in countries where grave human rights violations may occur. The curriculum provides for training in international humanitarian law and human rights law, as well as U.S. human rights law. It also reportedly includes role-playing on procedures for reporting discoveries or reports of human rights violations by foreign nationals. The new curriculum will be used for key personnel assigned to the embassy from the Departments of State, Treasury, Commerce, Defense (including all military attaches), as well as from the Coast Guard and the

---

[32] U.S. police training programs between 1962 and 1974, for instance, consistently stressed what today would be known as "human rights" or "community relations". See WOLA, Police Aid and Political Will, November 1987, pp. 8-9.

[33] For example, on June 2, 1982, Deputy Assistant Secretary of Defense (and later contra-supply networker) Néstor Sanchez told Congress, "The first quick-reaction battalion trained by U.S. instructors -- the Atlacatl battalion -- has achieved a commendable combat record not only for its tactical capacity in fighting the guerrillas but also for its humane treatment of the people." On IMET training for Guatemala, see testimony of Assistant Secretary of State Langhorne Motley, before Subcommittee on Western Hemisphere Affairs, March 5, 1985.

[34] See, for e.g., Joy Hackel and Daniel Siegel, In Contempt of Congress, op cit., where Amnesty International, human rights groups, Newsweek and The New York Times document U.S.-trained Atlacatl Battalion participation in massacres between 1982 and 1984. Members of the Atlacatl Battalion, with over six years of U.S. training, were responsible for the 1989 slaying of six Jesuits and two civilians. On broader evidence of the argument, see Lars Schoultz, Human Rights and U.S. Policy Toward Latin America, Princeton University Press, 1981.

[35] Personal interview, Quarry Heights, Panama, early 1991.

Drug Enforcement Administration.[36] However, while such training may be helpful for U.S. personnel, it does not affect those of the host governments.

Sixth, whatever the future benefits of engaging Andean militaries, the administration has refused to exercise any sort of public pressure on the government of Colombia to improve its human rights record. The administration has used its influence to lobby the Colombian government for the retention of extradition and for tough legal treatment of drug traffickers. Despite acknowledging "significant abuses" by members of the police and military," the State Department has said little about these abuses publicly. An official of the U.S. embassy in Bogotá said,

> Most of the impetus for human rights respect is coming from within Colombia -- the President, the Procurador, the population, the constituyente [Constituent Assembly] -- the country is committed to human rights... One can't exaggerate U.S. influence -- Colombians are proud. Their changes are coming about from internal pressures.[37]

When asked about the United States' actions on human rights in Colombia, another official of the U.S. embassy failed to cite any activities beyond monitoring agreements:

> It's naive to think that you can take someone who's grown up in this milieu where human rights have a completely different meaning and who's now 27 years old and turn them around -- it's beyond hope. But contact with the U.S. does help. Putting this [human rights] language in the agreements forces the commanders to recognize the importance of human rights. Hopefully increased exposure to this will inculcate some of these values. We monitor these agreements weekly. We are very insistent on respect for human rights..."[38]

The administration's 1991 determination on Colombia's human rights performance said, "The main source of the violence and of human rights abuses continues to be narco-traffickers and right- and left-wing extremist groups," without referring to the connection between the Colombian armed

---

[36] Unclassified inter-agency memorandum, State Department, "Inter-Agency Prototype Human Rights Course Outline, December 1990.

[37] Jochnick interviews, Summer 1991, op cit.

[38] Ibid.

forces and the paramilitary groups.[39] Far from threatening to cut assistance over ongoing human rights violations, or even from decrying publicly the need to establish military accountability and to end paramilitary activity, the U.S. administration has consistently pointed to improvements in the statistics or steps taken by the Colombian government.

In the case of Peru, the Bush administration acknowledges serious human rights problems, but has prioritized the "war on drugs" over the grave human rights situation. At U.S. insistence, human rights language has been incorporated into bilateral antinarcotics agreements with Peru. The U.S. ambassador has publicly stressed human rights, and, commendably, the State Department condemned and called for an investigation of the letter-bombing of the offices of Peru's respected non-governmental National Human Rights Commission, which resulted in grave injury to the director of the legal department.[40] The United States has also encouraged the Peruvian government to implement reforms that could lead to an improvement in Peru's human rights situation.

However, as with Colombia, the U.S. has cast its options as a choice between engaging the armed forces or remaining more or less disengaged from the armed forces.[41] Commendably, in September 1991, key congressional committees imposed a series of conditions on FY 1991 military aid to Peru, including consultation with Congress on progress in eight specific human rights cases, the publication of a central registry of persons detained by Peruvian security forces, and immediate access by Peruvian judicial officials and the International Committee of the Red Cross to all detention centers. In addition, Congress continued to withhold $10.05 million destined for the Peruvian army. However, the administration's highest priority in Peru has been to secure a bilateral anti-drug agreement whereby military aid might flow.

To this end, human rights criticisms have been muted in recent months. In a mid-1991 trip to Peru, for example, Assistant Secretary of State for Human Rights and Humanitarian Affairs Richard Schifter did not make a single public statement regarding the human rights situation in Peru. Indeed, the administration has at times seriously understated the Andean governments' role in human rights violations. In addressing concerns about human rights in a report required by Congress on the impact of antinarcotics programs on

---

[39] "Determination Under Section 4(a) of the International Narcotics Control Act of 1990," submitted by Secretary of State James Baker to Congress, January 25, 1991, p. 7.

[40] See statement by Richard Boucher, Deputy Spokesperson, U.S. State Department, March 19, 1991.

[41] Private conversations with State Department officials, mid-1991.

the Andean countries, the Departments of Defense and State did not mention ongoing violations, implying instead that such abuses were in the past.[42]

II. MILITARIZATION AND DEMOCRATIZATION

The Bush administration has underscored democratization as one of its foreign policy goals in the hemisphere. Secretary Baker stated in May 1991 that "promoting and consolidating democratic values" was the top objective of U.S. foreign assistance for the Bush administration.[43] Then-Deputy Assistant Secretary of Defense Nancy Dorn said in March 1991, "The challenge of the 1990s is to reinforce democratic institutions so they may withstand the pressures that have toppled them in the past."[44] In 1991, Gen. Joulwan upgraded "strengthening democratic institutions" from #2 to #1 in the list of SouthCom's overall strategic objectives.[45]

The administration claims not only that the Andean strategy will not harm democratization processes in the region, but that it will strengthen such processes. The administration points to the danger to democratization posed by traffickers and insurgents: "...the support of the military could be critical in maintaining the stability of Andean democracies against the pressure of narcotics traffickers and insurgents." In addition, the administration claims that "Current projected levels of U.S. assistance will not undermine the authority and control of civilian governments nor weaken democracy."[46] The administration gives five reasons why its military aid to the Andes "will help to strengthen democracy":

"(1)   U.S. security assistance details are developed through military-to-military contacts, but the policy outlines, negotiation and approval is through civilian government authorities;

"(2)   an impoverished, poorly trained and equipped military, unable to feed its troops, is far more susceptible to corruption and human rights abuses;

---

[42] See quote above: "We cannot gloss over **past** [human rights] abuses in some countries." (emphasis added)

[43] Secretary of State James Baker, "Foreign Assistance Funding Proposal for FY 1992," US Department of State Dispatch, May 27, 1991, p. 372.

[44] Hearings, "Review of the 1991 INCSR...," March 1991.

[45] Juan O. Tamayo, "From Battling Guerrillas to Pulling Teeth," The Miami Herald, June 14, 1991. For old priorities, see SouthCom's "Southern Theatre Strategy," February 12, 1991.

[46] From "Andean Anti-Drug Efforts: A Report to the Congress," submitted jointly to Congress by the Departments of Defense and State in fulfillment of Section 1009 of the Defense Authorization Act for FY 1991, February 1991, pp. 5-6.

"(3)   the military is far more likely to take a constructive approach if actively engaged in the drug war, as opposed to being left to criticize civilian efforts from the sidelines;

"(4)   the involvement of the military, as in the U.S., can bring a significant resource in the war against drugs if properly coordinated and directed by civilian authorities; and

"(5)   democracy cannot survive without the sound economic development which can only exist in a secure environment."[47]

The administration's stated concerns about democracy, and especially its new defense priorities, mark an unprecedented and welcome departure from past practices of making geo-political military interests the top priority U.S. security objectives in the region.

However, members of Congress, experts on Latin America, Andean government officials, and Andean non-governmental organizations are concerned that the Andean strategy will strengthen Andean militaries at a time when curbing military autonomy is critical to future democratization. Although conditions vary from country to country, these opinions corroborate what WOLA claimed when called to testify on this issue before Congress:

> In all three countries, the civilian governments' control of military forces is tenuous at best. In Peru and Colombia, increasing power has been ceded to the military in the name of maintaining public order. In Peru and Bolivia, the legacy of military rule looms over efforts to consolidate democratic transitions.   Under these circumstances, U.S. advocacy of involvement of Andean armed forces in domestic law enforcement operations...could severely jeopardize civilian control and democratic trends.[48]

Again, despite the broad congressional commitment to strong action in the drug war, Congress has also expressed concern about the Andean strategy's potential negative effects for democratization. In 1990, Congress conditioned drug-related security assistance on civilian control. Section 4(a) of the International Narcotics Control Act of 1990 requires the President to issue a determination that "the government of [the recipient] country has effective control over police and military operations related to counternarcotics

---

[47] Ibid.

[48] Testimony of Dr. Alexander Wilde, Executive Director, Washington Office on Latin America, before the Western Hemisphere Subcommittee of the House Foreign Affairs Committee, February 26, 1991, p. 5.

and counterinsurgency activities." In its November 1990 report, the House Government Operations Committee notes its concern that "militarization" may result in "strengthened, more independent and less accountable militaries at the expense of already weak democratic institutions throughout the region."[49] The Chairman of the House Western Hemisphere subcommittee, responding to the mid-1991 Presidential determination that civilian control exists in Peru, said that the Peruvian government had abdicated authority for its counterinsurgency campaign to the military.[50]

BOLIVIA

Experts and government officials of Peru and Bolivia have also expressed concerns about the effects of the Andean strategy on civilian control. Bolivian sociologist Raúl Barrios says, "Increasing the military's potential in Bolivia is a serious matter. By augmenting its autonomy, the United States may very well be breaking down the military's subordination to civilian powers."[51] Professor Eduardo Gamarra, a recognized expert on Bolivia, testified in 1990 that "Bolivia's efforts to consolidate democracy and promote economic growth, however, may well be torn apart by the very U.S. strategies offered to support them."[52] He and others underscore the Bolivian armed forces' long history of intervention into politics -- the country has experienced 182 military coups in its 166 years of independence. The latest round of military interventions was sparked in 1964 when, along with other factors, infusions of U.S. military aid to the Bolivian military strengthened the army's political position.[53]

While the country is now into its third consecutive civilian government, the military remains close to the halls of power. President Paz Zamora's MIR gained the presidency with the backing of the ADN, led by former dictator Hugo Banzer, whose support is essential for the government. Many military and police officials who held high posts during the most recent military regime of Gen. Luis García Meza (1980-81) are in positions of power, as are those involved in a 1984 coup attempt against President Siles Suazo, such as Col. Germán Linares, currently head of police intelligence. García Meza established a "narco-dictatorship" in which the cocaine trade, which had first developed during Banzer's rule, was consolidated under the

---

[49] "U.S. Anti-Narcotics Activities in the Andean Region," op cit.

[50] Representative Robert Torricelli, "U.S. Says Peru Making Progress in Human Rights," Reuters press wire, July 30, 1991.

[51] Quoted in Leslie Wirpsa, "U.S. Militarization of Antidrug Campaign in Bolivia Fires More Peasant Opposition," National Catholic Reporter, June 21, 1991.

[52] Hearings before the Western Hemisphere Subcommittee of the House Foreign Affairs Committee, "The Andean Initiative," June 6, 20, 1990, p. 49.

[53] Ibid., p. 57.

military. "In contrast to Argentina, Bolivia's military has not been brought to trial for corruption and human rights atrocities."[54]

Many experts have warned about the institutional effects of the military component of the Andean strategy on the Bolivian armed forces. Gamarra says,

> Involvement in the drug war by the armed forces, even through civic action programs, will inevitably increase its size and role. Their growth, at the expense of civilian institutions, cannot bode well for democracy in Bolivia.[55]

In fact, U.S. military aid is significantly boosting the resources allocated to the Bolivian military. U.S. military assistance in FY 1990 represented 41% of the total defense budget for that year. Since military assistance was withheld from the Bolivian army in 1990, the Air Force and Navy absorbed most of the aid. In the summer of 1991, about 2,000 of the army's total forces (20-27,000) will be trained by U.S. Special Forces Mobile Training Teams. In addition, the army will expand its civic action activities in the countryside, foregoing the opportunity to develop civilian institutional capabilities in favor of expanding the scope of military activities.

The U.S. Embassy in La Paz implicitly recognizes that its antinarcotics security assistance affects internal politics and civil-military relations in that country. Spokespersons for the U.S. embassy in La Paz have stated that the army's recently begun anti-drug training is necessary because U.S. assistance to Bolivian police forces has given the police better equipment than the army and new stature, sparking jealousy among the army. The administration claims that giving the army new equipment and a more privileged role will help "balance" the increased stature of the police. Bolivians fear that instead the aid will further fuel the strengthening of security forces at a time when institutionalization of civilian rule is in its early stages. One high-level Bolivian government official told WOLA, "Civilian power has already declined [due to militarization of the drug war]."[56]

Concern is also widespread about the corruption of the armed forces, which is seen as linked to civilians' ability to control the military. Gamarra

---

[54] Gamarra, op cit. The civilian governments have been unable to administer justice in the case of García Meza himself, despite a drawn-out trial for crimes committed during his rule. García Meza continues to move about freely in Bolivia and reportedly receives his military pension on a regular basis. Also Jonathan Marshall, Drug Wars: Corruption, Counter-insurgency and Covert Operations in the Third World, Cohan and Cohen Publishers, 1991, and Gamarra, op cit.

[55] Gamarra, hearings on "The Andean Strategy," op cit., p. 57.

[56] Personal interview, 1991. Official requested anonymity.

claims that "the corruption of the [military] institution is a foregone conclusion" given its participation in the drug war. One official of a peasant federation attributes some of UMOPAR's distaste for the army's involvement to the fact that "it could take business away from some UMOPAR agents."[57] Officials and others fear that the military's inevitable corruption once it gets involved in the drug war will be worse than the effects on the UMOPAR. "How Bolivian democracy will survive a corrupt military with ties to the drug industry is a question few are willing to ponder."[58] A former Planning Minister in Bolivia indicated the dangers of increased corruption for civilian control: "When you have a corrupt chief of police, you fire him. When you have a corrupt chief of the army, he fires you."[59]

PERU

Peru has just completed its second transfer of power from one civilian president to another. But for most of its history Peru has been under military rule, most recently between 1968 and 1980. The return to civilian rule corresponded, ironically, with the brutal Shining Path guerrillas launching its "armed struggle." In its efforts to stem the guerrillas, the civilian government has steadily expanded the military's power, creating a dual state divided between those governed by elected civilian officials and those living under strict military rule.

In December 1982, then-President Belaúnde shifted primary responsibility for combatting the Shining Path from the Sinchi police force to the Peruvian armed forces. He declared five provinces in the Ayacucho department to be "under a state of emergency," suspending basic civil liberties and placing authority in the hands of the military. Thus began the spiral of violence between the Shining Path guerrillas and the Peruvian security forces, with the local population -- mostly rural peasants -- caught in the crossfire.

Military control over the counterinsurgency strategy has increased since President Fujimori took office in July 1990. He has added provinces in Cuzco, Puno and Arequipa and the entire department of Ica to the areas declared "emergency zones," which as of August 1991 covered 40% of the

---

[57] Abel Roque, Federation of Peasants and Workers, Villa Catorce, Chapare, quoted in Wirpsa, op cit.

[58] Gamarra, hearings "The Andean Initiative," op cit., p. 59.

[59] Gonzalo Sánchez de Losada, quoted in Thomas Kahn, "Bolivians Fear a U.S.-led War on Drugs," The Wall Street Journal, June 24, 1991.

national territory and 55% of the country's population.[60] Fujimori appointed an active-duty military officer to head the Ministry of the Interior, effectively placing all of the internal security forces under increased military control, and he continued the practice of the García Pérez government of appointing an active-duty military general to head the Ministry of Defense.

Shortly after taking office, Fujimori proposed a series of measures that respond to long-standing demands of the military. Aimed at increasing the military's capability to fight Sendero, the proposals would curb civil and human rights and give the military an even freer hand in counterinsurgency activities. Late last year, Fujimori responded to the assassination of agronomist Javier Puiggrós (by the Shining Path) by proposing a constitutional reform to allow "suspected subversives" to be tried in military courts. Using powers granted by the Congress to issue presidential decrees, Fujimori limited the use of habeas corpus and decreed that military personnel in emergency zones could use pseudonyms to conceal their identities, further limiting public accountability.

Most disturbingly, on December 23, 1990 he issued a decree that military and police forces operating in emergency zones are on duty 24 hours a day, and therefore any acts committed are necessarily considered to be in the line of duty and subject to military rather than civilian courts. The military penal code only contemplates negligence and abuse of authority, and no military official has ever been convicted in a military court of a human rights violation. The Peruvian Congress was sufficiently angered by the attempt to institutionalize impunity that it overturned the presidential decree. The situation of impunity, however, continues.

Only a handful of police have been convicted for human rights violations. In addition, Peru's National Human Rights Coordinating Committee pointed to two recent incidents as evidence of the lack of effective control over police forces: "the shooting down of a commercial airplane by members of the national police and the extrajudicial execution of three youth after they were seen being taken away in a patrol car are clear indications of the profound lack of control over the police forces, evident every day."[61]

---

[60] Just before this report went to print, and as U.S. military aid was suspended pending U.S. congressional hearings on Peru's human rights record, the Fujimori government lifted some emergency zones. However, within three weeks, the area declared under a state of emergency zones had again been extended. The zones declared under a state of emergency continue to change frequently.

[61] Coordinadora Nacional de Derechos Humanos, letter to Ambassador Quainton, August 1, 1991, WOLA's translation.

COLOMBIA

The Andean strategy could have important ramifications for Colombia as well, although the potential U.S. impact on that country's internal politics is generally considered less than in other cases. Colombia's long history of civilian rule makes a military coup unlikely. In addition, a new constitution took effect in July 1991 which introduced significant reforms in a number of areas. An important step was also taken in August 1991, when President Gaviria named national security adviser Dr. Rafael Pardo to be the country's first civilian Minister of Defense in 35 years.

Nevertheless, Colombian academics and human rights monitors express concern that U.S. antinarcotics policy may contribute to a trend -- dating from the beginning of counterinsurgency campaigns in the 1960s -- toward increased military autonomy in matters related to internal and external defense.[62] Despite the new constitution's reforms, the new charter left intact the military's autonomy from civilian authority.[63] The Supreme Court ruled that no subject could be barred from consideration in the deliberations over the new constitution. But none of the major political forces dealt with the issue of stemming military powers or ongoing impunity for human rights violations. In fact, the only reform touching on the military as an institution extended its powers: the jurisdiction of military courts was extended to include police, despite the fact that such courts essentially guarantee impunity. One recommendation that would have altered the military court system was not accepted by the Constituent Assembly.[64] It is not clear the degree to which Pardo will (or can) broaden civilian control over military policy or curb impunity among the armed forces.

---

[62] This trend has been facilitated by the virtually continual "state of siege" over the past four decades and decrees limiting constitutional liberties. In addition, Colombia is the only country in South America in which the police force remains part of the Ministry of Defense, joining the internal and external security functions under military authority.

[63] The new constitution introduced significant electoral reforms designed to curb clientelism and which will likely end the three-decade-old bipartisan political regime. Some of the reforms related to civil-military relations include substantial judicial changes whose ultimate consequences will not be clear for some time and the alteration of "state of siege" decrees. With regard to the latter, one adviser to a Constituent Assembly leader said, "A substantial differentiation is made between a state of external war and one of 'internal commotion.' The latter may no longer be imposed indefinitely. It can be decreed for only 90 days, renewable by discretion only once and, with prior authorization by the Senate, for another 90 days. The temporary legislation issued by the President may not suspend civil liberties or basic rights; and the President will be responsible for any transgression committed in the exercise of state-of-emergency powers."

[64] The proposal read: "The Constitution and Colombian law should contain provisions that any complaint of extra-judicial, arbitrary or summary execution be promptly and impartially investigated by civilian judicial authorities and it should specify that perpetrators will be brought to justice." Colombia Human Rights Network, Colombia Update, July 1991, Vol.3; No. 3, p. 4.

The impact of U.S. policy is all the more important given the crucial juncture for the military's relationship to civilian authority in Colombia. Negotiations are presently underway with the two largest guerrilla forces -- the FARC and the ELN. However, in December 1990 the armed forces launched a major attack on the headquarters of the FARC guerrillas which many in Colombia interpreted as a sign of military opposition to the process of political reform and peace negotiations that were extended under President Gaviria. The media reported that Gaviria was unaware that the military had been planning to launch the attack. The lack of effective discipline over the military has been a critical obstacle throughout a series of peace talks with guerrilla factions initiated in 1982 and which under the Gaviria government have led to agreements with four former guerrilla groups. In the initial peace talks, the military openly opposed the process and hundreds of guerrillas who laid down their arms were killed. Reforms of the military and allied paramilitary groups is a key demand of the Simón Bolívar Guerrilla Coordinating body, which groups the principal organizations still opposing the government by force of arms.

Many Colombian experts are concerned that the Andean strategy will fuel military autonomy. One scholar reported that,

"Gaviria has made it clear that a civilian is needed in charge of the antinarcotics fight. The only way to give civilian institutions more power is to give them more assistance. If there's real concern for the civil-military balance, it's a joke to channel money through the military."[65]

One Colombian journalist said, "President Gaviria doesn't have the power to go after the military. He fears the military as do most Colombians."[66] One expert reported that "the military has increased its power through the drug war."[67] While a coup remains highly unlikely in Colombia, the Andean strategy could further undermine civilian oversight of counterinsurgency and other security policies, cementing the impunity of the Colombian armed forces.

III. FUELING VIOLENCE

In Peru, the military component of U.S. anti-narcotics policy is reported to have already fueled the growth of insurgent movements. Peruvian analysts

---

[65] Jochnick interviews, Summer 1991.

[66] Ibid.

[67] Jochnick interviews, Summer 1991, op cit.

claim that the Shining Path guerrillas have already benefitted from U.S.-backed eradication efforts. The guerrillas effectively play the role of "protector" of coca growers in the face of exploitative drug traffickers, on the one hand, and abusive police and military forces on the other hand. The lack of effective economic development alternatives for Peruvian coca growers whose livelihood is affected by eradication efforts has further aided the guerrillas' recruitment. In addition, the Shining Path guerrillas reportedly expect a nationalist backlash to the programmed expansion of U.S. training and advising roles which will work to their favor. Diego García-Sayán, Director of the Andean Commission of Jurists in Lima, testified in 1990, "Sendero Luminoso itself has said that they are expecting a greater U.S. presence in order to galvanize support for themselves as an 'anti-imperialist' force."[68] Tina Rosenberg, an expert on the Shining Path, echoed that warning:

> "[U.S. military assistance] could be 'gringo-izing' the war. Sendero has published numerous articles in its newspaper welcoming this possibility as an organizational tool. Sendero claims this would 'reveal the true nature of the conflict' and help the movement to recruit new members."[69]

The Néstor Paz Zamora Command (CNPZ) of the National Liberation Army and the FARC in Colombia have also effectively utilized repressive antinarcotics activities to gain the support of the local population. In an October 1990 communique, the CNPZ highlighted its opposition to U.S. drug policy in Bolivia. Bombs have exploded near the home of the U.S. ambassador and destroyed a statue of John F. Kennedy in La Paz. Thus, in all three countries U.S.-backed antinarcotics programs appear to provide political ammunition to insurgencies, adding further fuel to the fire of political violence.

Moreover, repressive antinarcotics operations may lead to violent confrontations between coca growers and security forces responsible for eradication and interdiction efforts. This possibility is most evident in Bolivia's Chapare, where violent confrontations between the UMOPAR and well-organized coca growers have occurred in the past. For example, on May 27, 1987 five peasants were reportedly killed by UMOPAR troops in Parotani, Cochabamba. In a widely-reported incident on June 27, 1989, UMOPAR troops opened fire on a crowd protesting outside its headquarters in Villa

---

[68] Diego García-Sayán, hearings before the Western Hemisphere Subcommittee of the House Committee on Foreign Affairs, "The Andean Initiative," June 6, 1990, p. 19.

[69] Tina Rosenberg, testimony before the Senate Foreign Relations Subcommittees on Western Hemisphere and Peace Corps Affairs and Terrorism, Narcotics Control and International Operations, June 28, 1990, p. 11.

Tunari. An estimated twelve persons were killed in the stampede away from the gunfire -- many others were wounded and arrested.

The arrival of U.S. trainers and the introduction of Bolivia's army into the drug war, long feared by coca growers, brought to the surface many of the fears of coca growers in that country. Despite the government's assurances that the army will participate only in logistical support operations and not actual operations, many coca growers believe that violent confrontation is now inevitable.[70] "Sooner or later the army will attack us directly," said Segundo Montevilla, a leader of the campesino union CSUTB after the trainers arrived.[71] Montevilla and other coca growers representatives called for the formation of self-defense groups which would be for defensive purposes only.[72] A coca growers' leader from the Chapare, Evo Morales, said, "We will defend our coca with our lives," and another coca grower said, "We have arms and machetes and we're ready to use them."[73]

Both U.S. and Bolivian military officials have stated that the army will act only in cocaine processing and trafficking areas outside of the Chapare such as the Beni and the Pando.[74] However, one diplomat in La Paz responded,

> "The Americans have set themselves a trap. They make a distinction between coca-producing areas where peasants are and drug traffickers. Well, guess what, guys? Don't you think the cocaine producers will move in there to protect themselves, just like the Palestine Liberation Organization moves into civilian areas?"[75]

The balloon effect, the displacement of drug trafficking from one place to another by repression, can operate within as well as between countries. It could have important implications not only for levels of cocaine supply but also for levels of violence.

---

[70] On the Bolivian army's role, see "No 'Direct Intervention' Planned in Drug Fight," La Paz Televisión Boliviana, Nov. 6, 1990, appearing in Foreign Broadcast Information Service, Nov. 7, 1990.

[71] Quoted in James Painter, "Bolivians Protest US Militarization of Drug War," The Christian Science Monitor, April 15, 1991.

[72] Painter, "Bolivians Resist U.S. Aid Terms," op cit.

[73] Ibid., and Thomas Kahn, "Bolivians Fear a U.S.-Led War on Drugs," The Wall Street Journal, June 24, 1991.

[74] Personal interview with Col. Keith Nightingale, SouthCom Counter-narcotics Chief, early 1991.

[75] Ibid.

CONCLUSION

The traffic in illegal drugs poses real dangers to society in the United States and in the Andes. It has bred criminal violence in both places that rends the social fabric, particularly among the poor in cities, and has exacerbated political violence, which strikes in the Andes against both civilian governments and uncounted victims innocent of anything except legal political expression. How much such violence is the result of the illegality of cocaine -- as distinguished from its intrinsic character -- is a matter of debate among experts. Much less debatable is the physical and moral damage of cocaine abuse, for individuals and communities, in the Andes as well as the U.S.

Drug trafficking has also undermined already-weak political institutions -- police, judges, political parties -- through corruption. The effects are visible in all three of the Andean countries, and increasingly elsewhere in Latin America: in Panama, where drug trafficking is reportedly flourishing despite the removal of Manuel Noriega; in Argentina, where members of the family of President Menem's wife have been indicted on money laundering charges; and in Western Brazil and Guatemala, where incidents of drug-related violence are on the rise. The existence of powerful international criminal cartels raises new dangers for a global order in the midst of fundamental flux. It is necessary and legitimate for national governments to respond to these serious problems, both individually and collectively.

However, the military remedy that the U.S. has chosen in the Andean strategy is an ill-conceived response. It shows no promise of ameliorating the problems of drug trafficking and addiction in U.S. cities by cutting the supply of cocaine coming from the Andes. Worse, it threatens human rights and fragile civilian governments there by strengthening national security forces that commit widespread abuses and operate beyond democratic control. And in so doing, it associates the U.S. government with abusive forces and extends U.S. military involvement into fundamental questions of internal security -- including ongoing armed insurgencies -- in the Andean societies.

These "clear and present dangers"[1] of current U.S. policy have not yet been faced in a public debate that is now imperative, both in the United States and in the Andes. What are the problems that policy fails to solve,

---

[1] The phrase was first used by Oliver Wendell Holmes, in his famous opinion that Congress should limit the free-speech protections of the First Amendment only when there was a "clear and present danger" of creating "substantive evils" without such limits (*Schenck v. United States [1919].*) It has been given more recent currency by the best-selling Tom Clancy novel by that title, about a CIA anti-narcotics operation run amok in Colombia. One military analyst reported to WOLA that a member of SouthCom, holding up Clancy's novel, said to him, "This is our Bible!"

1. U.S. abuse and drug-related violence. The single most important change for a more effective policy would be taking the U.S. drug problem seriously in its own terms. For drug abuse, the Bush administration has moved beyond "just say no," but its policy has not yet confronted the market logic of cocaine, which dictates shifting the focus of antinarcotics resources from the supply side to demand. Even if drug trafficking organizations could be successfully "disrupted" abroad, that in itself would not significantly affect drug consumption and drug-related violence in the United States. And even experts and administration officials who believe that supply-side efforts are effective acknowledge the need to channel more funds to treatment, education and prevention programs as the only way really to resolve drug-related social and health problems.

For drug-related crime and violence, as distinct from abuse, the U.S. would be more helpful to Andean countries if it were doing more to put its own house in order. This includes more serious debate about strategies of domestic law enforcement and the dangers to core constitutional liberties of a "war on drug-related crime." Furthermore, it remains true that the vast bulk of drug trafficking profits are made within the U.S. itself, rather than the Andes. It is widely believed among Andean officials and experts that the U.S. government has been too slow and ineffective in moving against money laundering through U.S. banks.[2] The U.S. appears to be requiring "political will" from Andean governments -- for which the economic benefits of the drug trade are very significant -- when it does not exhibit enough of that will itself.

2. Andean Priorities and "Political Will." A more effective policy would take Andean priorities more seriously. The U.S. can have a role in helping Andean governments confront the problems of drugs in their own societies, which include increasing addiction as well as corruption of their institutions and violence. But such a policy would need to address much more fully the nature of those problems in the region itself, which vary from one country to another. The starting point in constructing such an alternative policy would be much more attention to the opinions and interests both of governments and of nongovernmental actors concerned with these problems in the different countries. The Bolivian coca-growers, for example, understand the dangers they face from criminal violence, and have put forward proposals for viable alternative crops. Whatever the real difficulties in terms of U.S. domestic politics, a policy which genuinely aims to aid Andean countries with

---

[2] Rodrigo Uprimny, "The U.S. War on Drugs: Addicted to Repression?" WOLA International Drug Policy Briefing Series, Brief #1, December 10, 1990.

<u>their</u> drug problems must deal with the political and economic roots, and effects, of increased coca production.

Similarly, a more effective policy would take into account that, whatever "political will" of Andean governments have toward addressing their drug problems will be focused toward those problems as <u>they</u>, not the United States, conceives them. None of these governments gives anything like the priority assigned by the U.S. to fighting their part of the "war on drugs." Each of them faces an extraordinary array of other policy problems, and all have now accepted U.S. antinarcotics aid which may or may not help them tackle those problems. But the U.S. has not created -- and cannot create -- the kind of "political will" on which the U.S. drug strategy depends. Andean governments will always have their own assessments of what is politically viable concerning their own drug problems in light of interests and opinions within their own societies.

U.S. policy to date has made some concessions to Andean interests and sensibilities. Although the Bush administration largely conceived, designed, and initiated the Andean strategy on its own, it has to its credit moved away from eradication programs, included significant economic aid, and adopted a more multilateral tone (as in U.S. participation in the Cartagena Summit). But the U.S.-designed military strategy has remained the core of the policy, and the predominant dynamic has continued to be bilateral, with the U.S. wielding economic assistance in exchange for military cooperation with each of the three Andean governments in turn.

In particular, the U.S. has resolutely maintained its commitment to involving Andean militaries in the drug war in the face of the dangers of such a mission voiced by fragile civilian governments. With that involvement now initiated, the dangers remain -- as do the opportunities to avoid them.

3. <u>Law enforcement</u>. The criminal activities associated with drug trafficking have raised profound challenges of law enforcement for beleaguered Andean justice systems. U.S. aid to governments within the Andean Initiative includes components to assist their justice systems, including the police. Some of this aid -- to seriously understaffed court systems through Administration of Justice programs, for example -- does not pose the same risks as aid to police and military forces, and may help strengthen the rule of law.[3] It is the best way for the U.S. to support Andean governments confront their problems of law enforcement.

---

[3] *Elusive Justice* (WOLA, 1990) examines the development of U.S. Administration of Justice programs in the 1980s, with case studies of Guatemala, El Salvador, and Colombia. The report draws the broad conclusion that such aid is useful only in proportion to the reform commitment of recipient governments themselves.

From the perspective of strengthening democratic civilian government, aid to Andean police forces may seem more attractive than military training and assistance. All the governments in the region have created special paramilitary units within the police that are responsible for the vast majority of law enforcement actions against traffickers, including the bulk of cocaine seizures and dismantling of drug laboratories. The character and institutional mission of the police is much more appropriate for anti-narcotics enforcement efforts than the armed forces, in the Andes as in the U.S.

However, U.S. aid to Latin American police forces raises many of the same problems as aid to military forces. First, police efforts cannot ultimately be any more effective than those of the military in the face of continued demand in the United States, Europe and elsewhere. Law enforcement efforts will continue to be a "holding action" at best.

Second, Andean governments still face endemic police corruption in using the police to deal with the traffickers. These weaknesses are not remedied by also involving Andean militaries in the same antinarcotics activities, in "support" roles which the armed forces themselves fear will corrupt their institutions. This fear, shared by U.S. military officials in their anti-drug role, illustrates the perils of larger scale corruption in even more dangerous institutions.

Third and most importantly, police forces in all three countries engage in gross violations of human rights. Again, the United States has a moral - - and legal --- obligation not to give assistance to Andean police forces before they meet minimal standards of human rights and humanitarian law. Given the past record of U.S. police aid, police training is far more questionable than assistance to Andean judicial systems.[4]

4. Drug trafficking and Andean insurgencies. Of the three elected civilian governments that are part of the Andean Initiative, Colombia and Peru both face armed insurgencies. Bolivia does not. In the case of Colombia, the guerrilla threat is long-standing and part of a much larger and more complex panorama of violence, including that caused by the cocaine cartels. In Peru, the Shining Path guerrillas have gained strength throughout the last decade, undermining the infrastructure of the economy and the fundamental institutions of the political system. They have a powerful presence in the Upper Huallaga Valley, the largest region of coca production in the world, where they have working relationships with drug trafficking mafias. More than 20,000 Peruvians have died in their ten-year war against the state.

---

[4] WOLA, Police Aid and Political Will, op cit.

Of the three countries analyzed in this report, only Peru presents a situation with serious semblance to the "narco-guerrilla" theory that guides U.S. military thinking in the international war on drugs. The narco-guerrilla theory conflates counter-insurgency and anti-narcotics activities and appears to offer to U.S. policymakers the possibility of fighting "old" and "new" enemies at the same time, "two birds with one stone." But even in Peru, that theory fails to account for the strategic contradictions between fighting the drug traffickers and fighting the Shining Path. The Peruvian army cannot both combat the drug traffickers and win the "hearts and minds" of coca-growing peasants. As a key adviser to the Fujimori government, Hernando de Soto, notes, "our military tells us that militarizing the drug war will give Sendero an army of 250,000 farmers."[5]

Should the U.S. aid the Fujimori government in the war against Sendero? There is no doubt that it should support Peruvian efforts to resolve the country's deepening economic crisis and to promote equitable development. Indeed, pervasive poverty and inequality are at the root of political violence in Peru today and provide a fertile recruiting ground for the guerrillas. The accelerating impoverishment of the population now visible in urban areas is already accompanied by unprecedented Sendero activity there. Addressing these problems is crucial for the Peruvian government to cope more effectively with Sendero.

Military aid is another question. It deserves to be debated in its own terms, not disguised as part of a different war, the war on drugs. Without guarantees -- stronger guarantees than Peru has given to date -- that fundamental human rights will be respected by security forces, U.S. military assistance is, rightly, prohibited by law. The Jesuit murders in El Salvador in 1989 are only the most visible recent reminder that such assistance should not be given prior to meaningful institutional reform. If such aid is provided to a Peruvian army responsible for widespread and systematic abuse against the country's civilian population, it may well have the effect of depriving the Fujimori government of the greater popular support it needs to defeat Sendero. The deepest interests in U.S. policy toward Peru are protecting human rights and strengthening democratic government in that country.

U.S. SECURITY POLICY AND LATIN AMERICAN DEMOCRACY

Under the Bush administration, U.S. policy toward Latin America has taken a welcome turn away from outmoded Cold-War concerns and given new

---

[5] Personal interview, Washington, D.C., September 13, 1991.

emphasis to trade and investment. This policy is manifested in Bush's Enterprise for the Americas Initiative, the North American Free Trade Agreement negotiations with Mexico, and the Proposal for Democracy and Development in Central America. The Bush administration has also aimed to support the trend to elected civilian government in the region with an array of "democratic-assistance" programs (including Administration of Justice) that are administered by the Agency for International Development (AID) and the National Endowment for Democracy (NED) and its associated institutes.

These political and economic programs have echoes of President Kennedy's Alliance for Progress, in another era of developmental optimism. However, the Andean strategy analyzed in this report is also an important strand of the larger policy toward the hemisphere. And it recalls another key aspect of U.S. policy in the Alliance period: the parallel tracks of development assistance, on one side, and of military aid for counterinsurgency, on the other.

The Drug War lacks the profound political dimensions of the Cold War. Hence, it is unlikely to have the same potential to shape internal political conflict in Latin America or to structure U.S. policy toward the region. Nevertheless, as during the Alliance, U.S. policy is marked by deep contradictions. The military component of the "war on drugs" significantly threatens both human rights and broader democratization. Even without the same elements of geo-political and ideological competition that drove the Cold War, the militarized drug war can have coruscating consequences for the region. Its similarities to U.S. security policy during the Alliance for Progress are disturbing:

* It encompasses "counter-narcotics" activities that are indistinguishable in practice from those of counterinsurgency and Low Intensity Conflict

* It legitimates Latin American security forces in a fundamental internal security role, now directed at "new" enemies, and confirms them as actors in domestic politics

* It supports aid to Latin American security forces responsible for widespread violations of basic human rights, endemically unable to distinguish between armed rebellion and legal political opposition, and fundamentally unaccountable to democratic civilian authority

* It provides U.S. equipment and training to Latin American militaries in the name of greater "professionalization" and enhanced U.S. "leverage" prior to any meaningful institutional reforms

* It identifies fundamental U.S. security interests in the hemisphere with military solutions to internal problems

* It confirms the U.S. military's historic patterns of tutelage within direct military-to-military relations in the region

* It is unfolding as a multi-year plan, with bureaucratic momentum within the U.S. government -- but without adequate congressional debate or oversight

In 1960, on the eve of the "two-track" policy of the Alliance period, most of the countries of Latin America were governed by elected civilian governments. In the succeeding decades, one country after another fell under military dictatorships, often guided explicitly by doctrines of national security which justified destruction of all "internal enemies" by repression of all dissent. This terrible transformation, which had consequences still felt throughout Latin America today, had many causes -- most of them within the societies and institutions of the Latin American countries themselves. But the influence of the United States -- and particularly, U.S. security policy -- contributed to it.

Now, Latin America has again experienced a wave of democracy -- indeed, one unprecedented in scope throughout the region -- and the United States government has again embarked on a policy to strengthen Latin American militaries. There are certainly differences, in context and in content, between that earlier policy and the military strategy now unfolding through the international drug war, and some of the policy changes are positive. The Bush administration, for example, is introducing reforms in the training of Latin American military personnel, including components on human rights.

Other changes, however, carry sinister implications. One of those is the extraordinary enhancement of intelligence-gathering by both U.S. and national security forces in Latin America. DEA agents in the Bolivian jungle are now able to hook up via satellite to intelligence data banks in Washington, D.C., in just 120 seconds. Plans aim to train Latin American forces in new modes of intelligence-gathering and provide them with millions of dollars worth of the latest high-tech equipment. During Latin America's institutional military dictatorships, intelligence units were the source of the worst manifestations of state terror. The character of intelligence, and the uses to which it is put, depends fundamentally on whether or not those in command of it answer to democratic civilian authority. Such authority does not control Andean security forces today.

Another change which bodes ill is the growing U.S. role in the planning and coordination of Latin American military and police actions in the hemispheric drug war. Tactical Analysis Teams of U.S. military intelligence personnel and Special Forces personnel already plan the details of raids carried out by U.S. DEA agents and national military and police forces. It is a central principle of Low-Intensity Conflict to limit use of U.S. troops abroad, and the Bush administration resolutely maintains that the U.S. role will be restricted to support for national Latin American forces. But the "narco-guerrilla" theory conflates drug traffickers and guerrilla rebels, and in that confusion there is real potential for the United States to be drawn more deeply into internal wars, especially in Peru. More generally, this planning-and-coordination role potentially involves the U.S. in a police function throughout the hemisphere.

Thirty years ago the U.S. Southern Command accepted a mission directed toward counter-insurgency and Low Intensity Conflict in Latin America. Now, with the end of the Cold War and the rise of elected governments throughout the region, the United States stands at another critical juncture. Choices made now, as . 30 years ago, are likely to have enduring consequences, for Latin America as well as for U.S. policy toward the region.

The broader U.S. security vision for the hemisphere that lies behind the Andean strategy is still incipient. That strategy itself, however -- with a well-articulated five-year plan -- is now in place within the agencies of the U.S. government. It does represent a response by the U.S. military to "do something" about the drug problem, and it is natural that it conceives the solution in military terms. But military capabilities -- destruction of targets or enemies -- are the wrong tools for a fight against drug-related violence. Many within the Pentagon itself have argued strongly against this course. It would be wise to heed them now -- and seriously to examine the implications of the militarized policy now in place before it leads to still worse consequences, for human rights and democracy in the Andes and the rest of Latin America.

APPENDIX A
What is "Low-Intensity Conflict"?

The concept of low-intensity conflict (LIC) emerged out of the growing perception in U.S. foreign policy circles that the Cold War was being waged in the Third World through non-conventional guerrilla struggles, and that vital threats to U.S. security interests lay in the Third World. The term -- derived by the Pentagon itself -- draws on the U.S. military's "spectrum of conflict," ranging from "low-intensity" conflicts to "mid-intensity" conflicts (e.g., the Persian Gulf war) to "high-intensity" conflicts (e.g., World Wars I and II). The term is grounded in the U.S. viewpoint; for the parties involved low-intensity conflict can be a full-scale war. In practice, LIC is largely an ad hoc category that covers a range of activities including peacekeeping operations in Lebanon, counterinsurgency in El Salvador and elsewhere, pro-insurgency in Angola and elsewhere, the 1980 failed hostage rescue attempt in Iran, the bombing of Libya in 1986, and the invasion of Grenada in 1983.

Low-intensity conflict's most direct parent is the counterinsurgency theory that emerged in the early 1960s -- which itself was derived from pro-guerrilla strategies developed by the American OSS during World War II.[1] However, the U.S. military has engaged in anti-guerrilla warfare for many decades (e.g., against American Indians, in the Philippines at the turn of the century). Immediately following the Vietnam war, counterinsurgency fell out of favor with the Pentagon.

However, with the increasing involvement of U.S. military forces in counterinsurgency support and pro-insurgency support during the Reagan administration, "Low Intensity Conflict" attracted increasing attention in military thinking and doctrine. Conferences were held on the subject, and new manuals on low-intensity conflict were issued. Part of the increasing popularity of LIC doctrine in the 1980s reflected the "Vietnam syndrome" -- the deep reluctance both inside government and among the U.S. public to support large-scale U.S. interventions in Third World countries unless they are quickly resolved. LIC doctrine relies on national "proxy" forces wherever possible.

In 1986 the Army and Air Force created the Center for Low Intensity Conflict (CLIC). In 1987 a Board for Low Intensity Conflict was established at the National Security Council, and a new position called Assistant Secretary

---

[1] American counter-insurgency theory is itself drawn from French and British counter-insurgency doctrines. On low-intensity conflict, see also Michael Klare and Peter Kornbluh (eds.), Low Intensity Warfare, New York, Pantheon, 1988.

of Defense for Special Operations and Low Intensity Conflict was created. At the same time, a new unified command was created for Special Operations and low-intensity conflict, called the U.S. Special Operations Command, based in Florida.

The U.S. military has been, and continues to be, deeply divided over the significance of LIC doctrine. Even before the end of the Cold War, LIC proponents maintained that Third World countries were likely to become increasingly important to U.S. security, and that the chances of a conventional or nuclear conflict with the Soviet Union in the European theater were low. They argued that U.S. doctrine was excessively Euro-centric and that U.S. forces were inadequate to respond to the more probable scenarios of terrorist threats, wars of national liberation, and drug trafficking.

Opponents of LIC have argued against diverting resources from the country's more serious security threats -- nuclear and conventional threats from large powers such as the Soviet Union. They have also been concerned that the military not be dragged into more "Vietnams" which place military strategy at the mercy of politicians and which non-military federal agencies should be carrying out. In addition, low intensity conflict does not require the massive hardware and personnel that traditional security missions garner for the services.

Defining LIC

Definitions of LIC are numerous and are one locus of debate between LIC proponents and opponents. The following definition appears in the 1988 Army-Air Force Manual on Military Operations in Low-Intensity Conflict:

> Low-Intensity Conflict is a politico-military confrontation between contending states or groups below conventional war and above the routine, peaceful competition among states. It frequently involves protracted struggles of competing principles or ideologies. Low-intensity conflict ranges from subversion to the use of armed force. It is waged by a combination of means, employing political, economic, informational, and military instruments.[2]

This definition stresses LIC's view of war as not simply military, but as also political, social and economic. The Army and Air Force agree on four major

---

[2] Headquarters, Departments of the Army and of the Air Force, FM-100-20, AFM 2-XY, Final Draft, "Military Operations in Low-Intensity Conflict," July 1988, p. 1-1.

LIC operational categories: (1) counterinsurgency and insurgency, (2) combatting terrorism, (3) peacetime contingency operations, and (4) peacekeeping operations.[3]

While these categories encompass quick strike or rescue missions by elite units, the two central thrusts of LIC remain pro-insurgency efforts (also known as "unconventional warfare -- UW") and counterinsurgency (also known as "Internal Defense and Development--IDAD", within another basically coterminous category, "Foreign Internal Defense--FID"). Indeed, a separate debate exists in the military over which LIC missions should receive priority. Some argue that LIC's most important missions are anti-terrorist strikes or rescue missions, because they offer the possibility of quick victories without protracted Vietnam-like struggles. These people argue that nobody can perform such operations as well as the military (having in mind primarily the CIA). Others see these missions as peripheral to the central struggles in the Third World which threaten U.S. interests -- insurgencies which require support or suppression. Certainly issues of insurgency and counterinsurgency have attracted the most attention in military thinking and doctrine, and some critics see LIC only as an attempt to talk about counterinsurgency under a different name.

U.S. special operations forces (SOFs) are central to LIC strategies of all operational categories. Special operations forces, the U.S. military's elite commandos, include Army Special Forces (SFs, also called "Green Berets"), the "Delta Force", Army Rangers, psychological and civil affairs units, Navy SEAL units, the Air Force Special Operations Wing, and Marine amphibious units (MAUs). With the growing legitimacy of LIC in the 1980s, special operations forces were slated to almost double in number between 1981 and 1990, despite entrenched opposition to the development of elite units in the armed forces.[4] Military leaders have traditionally opposed elite units because they strip regular forces of their best personnel and skew promotion processes.

Congress has taken the lead in institutionalizing special operations forces and low-intensity conflict. On the initiative of Senator Sam Nunn (D-GA), Congress forced the creation of a new Assistant Secretary of Defense for Special Operations and Low-Intensity Conflict (SO/LIC). Later, after DOD did not provide the bureau with what Congress thought were sufficient

---

[3] Ibid. Also see "A CLIC Report," Army-Air Force Center For Low Intensity Conflict and other documents.

[4] Stephen D. Goose, "Low-Intensity Warfare: The Warriors and their Weapons," in Klare and Kornbluh, op cit., p. 82.

resources, Congress legislated a separate budget and an increase in personnel for the new bureau.

APPENDIX B

Annex III: U.S.-Bolivian Counter-Narcotics Program
May 1990
Official English Text, Reproduced

Expanded Bolivian Armed Forces Participation

References:

A. United Sates Bolivian Agreement on Furnishing of Defense Articles and
    Services, April 26, 1962 (TIAS 5197).
B. Counter-Narcotics Program Agreement dated February 24, 1987.
C. Exchange of Notes dated December 23, 1988, Extending and Amending
    the Counter-Narcotics Program Agreement.
D. Annex I, Interdiction Project (dated December 23, 1988).
E. Annex II, Coca Reduction and Alternative Development Project (dated
    December 23, 1988).
F. The Cartagena Declaration, February 15, 1990.

I. Introduction

A. The Governments of the Republic of Bolivia and the United States of
    America (hereinafter "the Governments") concluded an Agreement on
    April 26, 1962, concerning the furnishing of defense articles and services
    to the Government of Bolivia for the purpose of contributing to its
    internal security capabilities.

    The Governments are agreed that production of and trafficking in illegal
    narcotics, by their very nature and by their direct violation of the laws
    of both countries, constitute a danger to internal security.

    For this reason the Governments agree to institute a special program for
    the special transfer of defense articles and services for the purpose of
    enhancing the capabilities of Bolivia's Armed Forces to participate in
    counter-narcotics actions as described in this Annex. This program will
    be put into operation in accordance with the sovereign interests of
    Bolivia, within its own legal procedures and constitutional provisions,
    under the authority of the President of the Republic of Bolivia, who will
    decide on the manner and timing of participation of the armed forces in
    conformity with the principles contained in the Cartagena Agreement
    dated February 15, 1990, which states: "The control of illegal trafficking
    in drugs is essentially a law enforcement matter. However, because of
    its magnitude and the different aspects involved, and in keeping with the

sovereign interest of each State and its own judicial system, the armed forces in each of the countries, within their own territory and national jurisdictions, may also participate. The Parties may establish bilateral and multilateral understandings for cooperations in accordance with their interests, needs and priorities."

B. The program described in this Annex shall be implemented in accordance with the terms of the Agreement of April 26, 1962 and Law 1008 on the regime of Coca and Controlled Substances. The Governments are agreed that, in accordance with paragraph 4 of the 1962 agreement, the defense articles and services furnished in implementation of this program are furnished for the exclusive purpose of enhancing the capabilities of Bolivia's Armed Forces in accordance with paragraph A above. The Government of the Republic of Bolivia accordingly will not permit the use of such articles or services for any other purpose.

C. The Governments entered into a basic Counter-Narcotics Program Agreement on February 24, 1987, which has been revised periodically, to provide a bilateral program of mutual support to combat narcotics trafficking. The original agreement provided for two Annexes, I and II, detailing projects for Interdiction, as well as Coca Reduction and related Alternative Development, respectively.

D. The Governments commit themselves to implement the counter-narcotics program described in the Annex in a manner of mutual support to those provided for under Annexes I and II. Details of the working and organizational relationship between the Special Force for the Fight Against Narcotics Trafficking provided for in Annex I and augmented Armed Forces involvement provided in Annex III will be describe in a note of Agreement to be executed at some future date.

II. Program Development and Organization for the Provision of Defense Articles and Services for Counter-Narcotics Purposes.

A. Subject to appropriation and availability of funds the United States Government agrees to provide defense articles and services valued at up to Thirty-Three Million Two Hundred and Twenty Eight Thousand U.S. Dollars (US$33,228,000.00) in Military Assistance Program Funds (FMF), from Fiscal Year 1990 funding to the Government of Bolivia and as a compliment to support provided for in Annex I. This includes a substantial civic action program. The level and nature of support for any project referred to in the execution of this program will be provided in detail in Letters of Offer and Acceptance or in Notes of Agreement between the authorized officials of the United States Government and the authorized Bolivian Government Officials receiving the articles and services.

B.   The Governments mutually agree that Fiscal Year 1990 funding may be used to initiate and support the types of units or projects identified in Subparagraph D. It is recognized that some projects are long-term in nature and may not be fully completed or fully developed during the first year. Future provision of defense articles and services provided by the United States Government, however, for the program as a whole or for any element thereof will be based on:

--The availability of funds provided by the United States Congress.
--The process shown in attaining objectives of this program, both by the timely rendering of this cooperation as well as by the accomplishment of the missions of support or participation, assigned to the Bolivian Armed Forces.

The effectiveness of any given counter-narcotics program or project will define the flow of requirements and the assistance as may be determined through agreed upon terms contained in Letters of Offer and Acceptance or in Notes of Agreement.

C.   In accordance with the statements of Section III, a), 2 of Annex I, the coordination between the Bolivian Armed Forces and the Special Anti-narcotic Force, will be described in implementing notes.

D.   The Governments agree that Bolivian Armed Forces counter-narcotics actions or projects supported during United States Fiscal Year 1990 may include the following:

    1.   For the National-Level, Joint Service Counter-Narcotics Infrastructure Development:

        a. A Counter-Narcotics Joint Operations Center.
        b. A Combined Joint Intelligence Center.
        c. A long-range Communications Net.
        d. A Communications Company.
        e. A Public Information Section.
        f. A Counter-Narcotics Training Center.
        g. A medical Company.

d. A Communications Company.

e. A Public Information Section.

f. A Counter-Narcotics Training Center.

g. A medical Company.

2.   Bolivian Armed Forces Requirements

a. Bolivian Army

-- Equip and train two Light Infantry Battalions for counter-narcotics operations.
-- Equip and train one Engineer Battalion for civic action.
-- Equip and train a Transportation Battalion.
-- Equip and train one Supply and Service Section.

b. Bolivian Air Force

-- Upgrade/augment helicopter, C-130, and other maintenance facilities, taking into consideration Hangar Number Three of the FAB Maintenance Center, Cochabamba.
-- Up to six additional UG-1H helicopters to the counter-narcotics "Red Devils" Helicopter Task Force Squadron, Group 51, in Cochabamba.
-- Periodic Depot Maintenance (PDM) on up to three c-130A aircraft currently in the Bolivian Air Force inventory and/or provide up to four C-130B aircraft.
-- Recondition and/or repair one FAB Casa 212.
-- Recondition, repair and upgrade up to four fixed-wing aircraft for light reconnaissance.
-- Jointly install and test a mobile radar unit in the Chapare to evaluate future effectiveness of such systems.
-- Develop a contract to repair and arm up to ten PC-7 aircraft.
-- Recondition and/or repair up to six T-33 aircraft.
-- Develop a contract to obtain, repair and/or send up to ten AT-33 aircraft.
-- Equip and train one Supply and Service Section.
-- Equip and train up to one Company-sized Air Military Police Unit for aviation physical security.

c. Bolivian Navy

-- Construct a support/repair facility at Puerto Villarroel for patrol boats and other surface units and a boat ramp.

-- To look for, try to obtain, and /or improve an appropriate vessel to be used as a hospital ship for civic action and medical support for counter-narcotics units.

-- Equip and train a Supply and Service Section.

-- Equip and train a Marine Infantry Company for riverine operations.

-- To equip personnel on boats and the boats themselves with lifesaving and repair equipment.

III. Mutually-Agreed, Expanded Counter-Narcotics Role, Missions, and Coordination for the Bolivian Armed Forces.

A. The Bolivian Armed Forces will utilize the resources provided by the United States Government, within the frame of provisions as described in this Annex III, in accordance with Bolivia's Law 1008 on the Regime of Coca and Controlled Substances, the Cartagena Declaration and subject to Bolivian legal procedures.

B. The Bolivian Armed Forces, within their available means, will supply the necessary personnel and basic facilities, and to the extent possible, resources for counter-narcotics operations to be conducted. It is agreed that transportation or other services in support of counter-narcotics missions provided by units receiving defense articles and services under this program shall be provided without financial cost except as the Governments may otherwise mutually agree.

C. Bolivian Armed Forces professional or career personnel, not including conscripts, who receive United States Government-funded training under this program will be assigned to or serve in units supported by this program for no less than two years upon completion of training unless mutually agreed upon by both Governments or otherwise removed for justifiable reasons.

D. The Bolivian Armed Forces will establish and maintain a close working and mutually supportive liaison and coordination with CONALID and the institutions of which it is formed, including the Sub-secretariat for Social Defense. At the national level, mutually supportive liaison may be accomplished through the exchange of appropriate staff liaison officers and through participation in an all-service (Army, Air Force, Navy, S.F.F.A.N.T., Ministry of Agriculture, etc.) Combined Joint Intelligence Center.

E. A rigorous selection process will be exercised in assigning personnel to units engaged in this counter-narcotics program, ensuring that those persons assigned to such units have no previous record of illegal involvement with narcotics production or trafficking. Any person assigned to such a unit who would have engaged in criminal acts will be immediately submitted to appropriate military or civil authorities in accordance with military regulations or Bolivian legal procedures.

F. Primary missions of the units assigned to the fight against narcotics trafficking could have the following characteristics:

1. Operations as described below will tend to preserve and improve the security conditions of the inhabitants, especially of those areas near to any of the places where the following operations will take place.

2. Continue supporting the Special Force of the Fight Against Narcotics Trafficking with established Aviation and Riverine Task Forces supported under Annex I.

3. The conduct of previously authorized operations against objectives such as the following: arms caches; processing laboratories of cocaine and its sub-products; collection points of controlled substances; illicit chemical precursors; seizure of narcotics trafficker assets; clandestine airstrips; aircraft involved in illicit drug trafficking, and other means used by narcotics traffickers.

4. Operations will also include: the conduct of air reconnaissance over areas which are hard to reach through other means, where it is reported illicit activities related to production and trafficking in narcotics drugs are being carried on.

5. Continue controlling waterways, including development of an information system relating to illicit traffic conducted using these waterways.

6. As part of alternative development, conduct civic action operations in narcotics affected areas and in other depressed areas of the national territory cooperating against narcotics trafficking, including road improvement, well drilling and irrigation, construction and repair of civic facilities, the provision

of humanitarian medical and dental assistance, and conduct counter-narcotics information campaigns.

7. Provide air transport for material, units, and personnel engaged in counter-narcotics operations as well as medical evacuation.

IV. Assessment of progress

A. Assessment of progress to achieve these goals will be conducted periodically. The objective of these reviews will be to assess the progress in achieving the effectiveness measures as defined in Paragraph II. B. of this Annex, to identify difficulties or shortcomings in program implementation, and to define future development of this program. As provided in paragraph 6 of the Agreement of April 26, 1962, such assessment will address all activities conducted under this Annex, as well as implementation in its entirety. The continued provision of assistance by the United States as well as the expanded Bolivian Armed Forces participation will depend upon this evaluation of the activities of the units and elements charged with the implementation of this program.

V. Standard Provisions

A. Title of all property delivered to the Government of Bolivia or its authorized representatives under this Annex shall be held by the Government of the Republic of Bolivia, unless otherwise specified in the applicable procurement documents.

B. As provided in paragraph 7 of the Agreement of April 26, 1962, the Government of the Republic of Bolivia will offer to return any articles, if deemed appropriate, furnished under this Annex by the Government of the United States of America that area no longer needed for the purpose for which furnished.

C. (1) Any foreign contractor, including any consulting firm, any foreign personnel of such contractor financed under the program, and any property or transaction related directly to such contracts, and

(2) any commodity procurement transaction financed under the program, are exempt from identifiable taxes, tariffs, duties, or other levies imposed under laws in effect in Bolivia and the United States of America.

D. The Government of Bolivia shall make such arrangements as may be necessary so that funds introduced into Bolivia by the United States

Government for purposes of carrying out obligations of the United States under this program shall be convertible into Bolivian currency at the rate of exchange which , at the time the conversion is made, is valid in Bolivia.

E. The Governments shall expend funds and support operations pursuant to this program only in accordance with the applicable laws and regulations of the United States and Bolivia, respectively.

F. As provided in paragraph 6 of the Agreement of April 26, 1962, the Government of the Republic of Bolivia will, as the United States may require, permit continuous observation and review by, and furnish necessary information to, representatives of the United States Government with regard to the use of defense articles and services provided under this Annex.

G. Each party will assign fully qualified personnel to participate in the monitoring and evaluation process. Each party will furnish the other with available, pertinent information as necessary to evaluate the effectiveness of program operations under the terms of this Annex. At the termination of the program, a completion report shall be issued as an integral part of this process. The completion report will include a summary of United States and Bolivian program contributions, provide a record of activities performed, objectives achieved, and related basic data.

H. Bolivia and the United States may request the assistance of other international organizations or public an private agencies in carrying out their respective obligations under this program.

VI. Definitions: As used in this Annex:

A. "Notes of Agreement" are documents which detail, clarify, and implement the terms and conditions of the Basic Agreement and Annex I or III. These Notes, which will be issued as often as necessary by competent agencies and the parties to the agreement, will in no way modify the substance of the basic agreement and Annex I or III; rather, they will clarify and provide guidance to facilitate implementation of the purposes of the agreement. Generally, such Notes will set forth:

1. Identification of:
   -- Official name
   -- Strength

-- Unit structure
-- Unit location

2.   the mechanisms and procedures to be followed in the course of program implementation;

3.   documents and reports which the Government of Bolivia must furnish to the United States Government to evaluate progress, compliance, and current fiscal status and accountability;

4.   establishment of detailed implementation plans;

5.   guidance on planning and organizing program activities;

6.   coordination of supply mechanisms.

B. "Letter of Offer and Acceptance" (LOA) means U.S. Department of Defense (DD) Form 1513 Offer and Acceptance by which the U.S. Government offers to sell to a foreign government or international organization defense articles and defense services pursuant to the Arms Export Control Act, as amended. The DD Form 1513 lists the items and/or services, estimated costs, the terms and conditions of sale, and provides for the foreign government's signature to indicate acceptance.

C. "Law 1008" is the Law of the Regime of Coca and Controlled Substances, dated July 19, 1988, as published in the Gaceta Oficial de Bolivia, Number 1558, on July 22, 1988.

D. The Cartagena Declaration is the document signed by the Presidents of the United States, Bolivia, Colombia and Peru on February 15, 1990.

APPENDIX C

MEMORANDUM OF UNDERSTANDING BETWEEN THE GOVERNMENTS OF THE UNITED STATES AND PERU CONCERNING COOPERATION IN COUNTERNARCOTICS ACTIVITIES
Official English Text, Reproduced

On May 14, 1991, the Government of Peru and the Government of the United States of America signed an agreement on Drug Control and Alternative Development Policy, in which both countries agreed to implement a joint venture. The structure of this joint venture must be constituted within six months of the date of signing. It is charged with the design and implementation of a new drug control policy, given that the previous policy in force to date, has not produced expected results, as agreed by both countries in the referenced May 14 Agreement.

Furthermore, during the six months foreseen for establishing the joint venture, both governments must continue adopting measures to enhance law enforcement and other actions against narcotics trafficking, as stated in paragraph 48 of the May 14, 1991 Agreement, within the Cartagena Declaration of February 15, 1991.

The Government of the United States and the Government of Peru (hereinafter "the Parties"):

Recognizing that the Parties have a common interest in attacking the causes of trafficking in narcotics by providing the necessary instruments to achieve a substantial reduction in or total elimination of the illegal cultivation of the coca-leaf and the marketing of the basic paste of cocaine in Peru;

Considering that cooperation between the Parties to attack the causes of such trafficking is based on policies of alternative development, security, interdiction, prevention within the context of a structural adjustment that creates appropriate conditions for the efficient functioning of a market economy in the Peruvian coca belt, with the special emphasis on preservation of the ecology;

Recognizing that in certain areas, counter-narcotics activities are threatened by subversive groups whose activities impede effective government action to combat narcotics trafficking, and whose activities are inextricably intertwined with those of the narcotics, and that, in those instances, counterinsurgency actions are a justifiable component of counter-narcotics activities;

150

Noting the authority of the President of the Republic of Peru to decide on the manner and timing of participation of the Peruvian armed forces in support of counter narcotics activities, in conformity with the principles contained in the Cartagena Agreement dated February 15, 1990.

Considering that as part of alternative development, police and military units may conduct civic action operations in narcotics affected areas, including road improvement, well drilling and irrigation, construction and repair of civil facilities, and the provision of humanitarian medical and dental assistance, and counter-narcotics information campaigns; and

Attaching great importance to implementing the objectives of this Agreement in a manner that is in accordance with internationally recognized standards of human rights behavior by respecting, inter alia, prohibitions against extra-judicial executions, disappearances, torture, arbitrary arrest and detention, and that require proper care for the sick and wounded;

Having reached the following understandings which the Parties intend to guide their cooperation:

ARTICLE I

1. The Government of Peru proposes, with the effective cooperation of the Government of the United States of America, to dismantle the clandestine laboratory infrastructure and transportation system used by narcotraffickers; reduce the amount of persecutors and chemical substances reaching narcotraffickers; and identify, disable and dismantle major cocaine production or distribution organizations through targeting and sustained investigations of major traffickers.

2. The Parties agree that in order to effectively support the attack on the narcotics threat and defend the sovereignty of Peru, the capabilities of the Peruvian Armed Forces must be able enhanced and training intensified. The Peruvian Armed Forces must be able to assure and reinforce civilian government control over the most important coca growing and trans-shipment areas, provide protection to police forces in counter-narcotics operations from the guerrilla
insurgents, and develop the capability to strike at drug trafficking organizations.

3. The Government of the United States of America proposes to provide training and equipment to enhance the ground, air and riverine counter-narcotics abilities and effectiveness of Government of Peru police and military

151

units assigned to support counter-narcotics activities. Monitoring of training and equipment provided by the Government of the United States of America for counter-narcotics purposes will be undertaken in accordance with existing agreements and practices.

4. The Parties understand that any funds provided through this memorandum for police and military counter-narcotics operations will be used exclusively to train, equip and deploy specialized counter-narcotics units and counter-narcotics support units, with the Upper Huallaga Valley of Peru as the principal area of focus.

5. The Parties will ensure that all those in command of military personnel, police or trainees will be held accountable for the conduct of those under their command and promptly investigate reports of human rights abuses.

6. The Parties recognize the importance of adhering to internationally recognized standards of human rights, to include providing access to detention facilities throughout Peru to appropriate international organizations.

ARTICLE II

1. The Government of the United States of America proposes to make available to the government of Peru up to $34.9 million to finance the purchase of U.S.-origin defense articles, defense services, and design and construction services under U.S. government letters of offer and acceptance to support those counter-narcotics activities in Peru which are delineated in article I, paragraph 4 of this agreement.

2. The parties agree that all the funds referred above in this Agreement to be provided by the United States to this effort will be subject to an annual evaluation requiring reduction of drug production and trafficking, sustained economic policy performance and respect for human rights, and the availability of funds appropriated by the Congress of the United States, and to the mutual agreement of the parties to proceed at the time of such availability.

ARTICLE III

The Parties intend to act in accordance with the aforementioned understandings. The Parties may agree on such legal undertakings as are necessary in order to achieve the goals and objectives set forth herein.

ARTICLE IV

This memorandum of understanding will become effective upon signature and shall remain in effect for one year. It may be amended by written agreement of the Parties.

In WITNESS WHEREOF, the undersigned, being duly authorized by their respective Governments, have signed this Memorandum of Understanding.

Done this 23 day of July, 1991, in both the English and Spanish languages, both texts being equally authentic.

FOR THE GOVERNMENT OF PERU:

Name: Carlos Torres y Torres Lara
Title: Prime Minister and Minister of Foreign Relations

FOR THE GOVERNMENT OF THE UNITED STATES OF AMERICA:

Name: Anthony C.E. Quainton
Title: Ambassador

APPENDIX D

U.S. ARMY SCHOOL OF THE AMERICAS
TOTAL ATTENDANCE, SELECTED COUNTRIES
1985-1990

	'85	'86*	'87	'88	'89	'90
COLOMBIA	363	488	613	547	469	402
BOLIVIA	50	17	24	28	64	220**
PERU	22	28	2	30	18	31
EL SALVADOR	369	349	269	583	646	312
ALL OTHERS	272	370	279	287	386	317
TOTALS	1076	1252	1187	1475	1583	1282

* The School of the Americas was moved from Panama to Ft. Benning, GA in 1986.
** Includes 81 Bolivian police and military personnel trained in an INM-funded program.

Source: Close-Out Reports 1985-1990, Directorate of Training and Doctrine, U.S. Army School of the Americas.